Techno Cozies

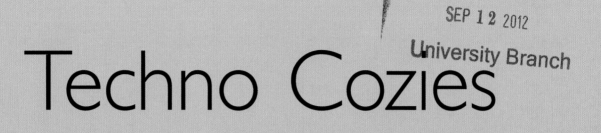

SUE CULLIGAN

Techno Cozies

GUILD OF MASTER CRAFTSMAN PUBLICATIONS

First published 2011 by
Guild of Master Craftsman Publications Ltd
Castle Place, 166 High Street,
Lewes, East Sussex BN7 1XU

Text © Sue Culligan, 2011
Copyright in the Work © GMC Publications Ltd, 2011

ISBN 978-1-86108-871-0

A catalogue record for this book is available from
the British Library.

Pattern checking by Sarah Hatton
Charts and project illustrations by Sue Culligan
Technique illustrations by Simon Rodway
Photography by Andrew Perris, except for
step-by-step shots by Sue Culligan

Publisher: Jonathan Bailey
Managing Editor: Gerrie Purcell
Production Manager: Jim Bulley
Senior Project Editor: Dominique Page
Editor: Judith Chamberlain-Webber
Managing Art Editor: Gilda Pacitti
Designer: Ginny Zeal

Set in Gill Sans
Colour origination by GMC Reprographics
Printed and bound by Hing Yip Printing Co. Ltd in China

Why we love techno cozies

MODERN TECHNOLOGY HAS TAKEN OVER OUR LIVES and everyone from kids to grannies now possesses at the very least a mobile phone. This unique collection of covers and cozies for all your technical gadgets will inspire knitters and stitchers alike.

The patterns are designed to encourage readers out of their comfort zone – if you are a knitter and have never tried crochet or sewing then give it a go, and vice versa. You will be amazed at just how easy it is to master a new craft.

The 30 colourful designs include cozies for laptops, cameras, mobiles, MP3 players and much more. They range from cute to luxurious – there is even a really useful one for your remote controls. The measurements given are for standard sizes, but these can easily be adapted to fit different models and you will find that some will double up for different gadgets. The finished projects make fabulous gifts for family and friends or you can just treat yourself.

Contents

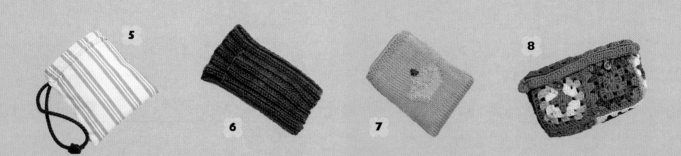

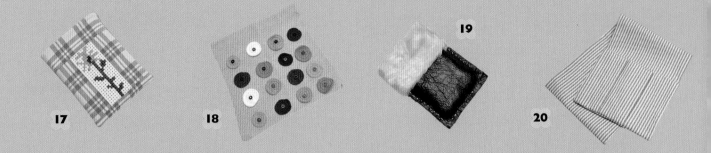

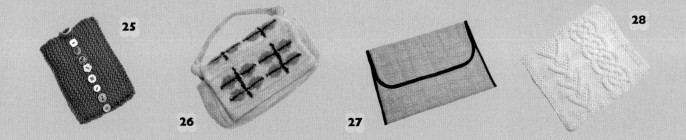

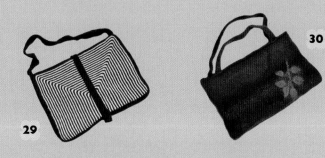

This attention-grabbing iPad cozy is created by a series of flaps fastened with Velcro strips. The simple appliqué is machine stitched to create a Union Jack flag on the front flap.

Union jack

Materials

13 x 35in (33 x 89cm) piece of medium-weight denim fabric x 3
10 x 19¾in (26 x 50cm) piece of gold felt
9 x 15in (23 x 38cm) piece of red felt
13 x 35in (33 x 89cm) piece of navy quilted lining fabric
10in (26cm) Velcro cut into 4 pieces measuring 2½in (6.5cm) each
Dressmaker's chalk
Straight-edge rule

Finished size

Approx. 12½ x 14in (32 x 35.5cm)

Front flap, base and bottom flap

1 Take one piece of the denim fabric; place it right side down on a table. Fold down the top 10in (26cm) so that the right side is facing to make the front flap.

2 Using the chalk and straight edge, cut two strips of gold felt measuring 19 x 2in (48 x 5cm) and lay diagonally across the front flap.

3 Pin in place, trimming the edges flush with the denim fabric, and machine stitch in place using satin stitch around all the raw edges.

4 Cut a piece of gold felt measuring 10 x 2in (26 x 5cm) and lay vertically down the centre of the cross. Pin in place and stitch as before.

5 Cut 4 pieces of red felt measuring 7 x 1in (18 x 2.5cm). Lay these on top of the gold cross, leaving a wider band of gold at the top of the left-hand diagonals and a wider band of gold at the bottom of the right-hand diagonals. Pin in place and stitch as before.

6 Cut a piece of gold felt measuring 15 x 4in (38 x 10cm) and lay it horizontally across the centre of the cross. Pin in place and stitch as before.

7 Cut 2 pieces of red felt measuring 1½ x 10in (4 x 25.5cm) and 3 x 15in (8 x 38cm). Lay the narrower piece on top of the vertical gold stripe, pin and stitch in place, then lay the wide red stripe across the horizontal gold band and stitch in place as before.

8 Lay the piece of fabric just completed right sides together with another piece of the denim fabric. Pin and stitch a ½in (1.5cm) seam down each long edge and across the short end with the appliqué. Turn right side out, poking out the corners with a pencil or knitting needle. Turn in the raw edges of the remaining seam, hand sew and press all the seams.

Side flaps and inner base

9 Place the remaining piece of denim fabric and lining fabric right sides together; pin and stitch around the two long edges and one short edge. Turn right side out and push out the corners. Turn in the raw edges of the remaining seam, hand sew and press all the seams.

Joining together

10 Place the fabric with the Union Jack right side down, then lay the piece of fabric horizontally across this, lining facing up. Place it so that it fits snugly against the fold line of the front flap; this will form where the appliqué finishes.

11 Pin the two pieces of fabric together where they meet to form a rectangle in the centre. Stitch all four sides of this square.

Finishing off

Place the cozy right side down with the appliqué at the top. Fold the left square inwards across the base square, and the right-hand square inwards on top of this one; attach a piece of Velcro to fasten

these at the left-hand edge of the cozy. Fold the bottom square upwards and attach a piece of Velcro to the top edge of this and the square beneath. Fold the top flap down and fasten the two

remaining pieces of Velcro in each corner of the flap and on the front flap of the cozy to fasten.

This unique laptop cozy was inspired by fronds of trailing seaweed. It was made from a recycled waistcoat and embellished with free-form knitted shapes in the beautiful shades of the Japanese Noro yarns.

Seaweed

Materials

Pure wool sweater, cardigan or waistcoat
(not machine washable)
2 x 50g balls of Noro Kureyon (plus 1 extra
ball if making pockets)
A pair of 4mm (UK8:US6) needles
2 large press studs
2 small press studs

Finished size

Approx. 17 x 14in (43 x 36cm)

Note

The garment used was an old waistcoat with two pockets. If the item you are felting does not have pockets, knit two square patches in stocking stitch measuring approximately 6 x 6in (15 x 15cm) in the Noro Kureyon, wash them and sew onto the front of the cozy to make pockets.

Measurement diagram

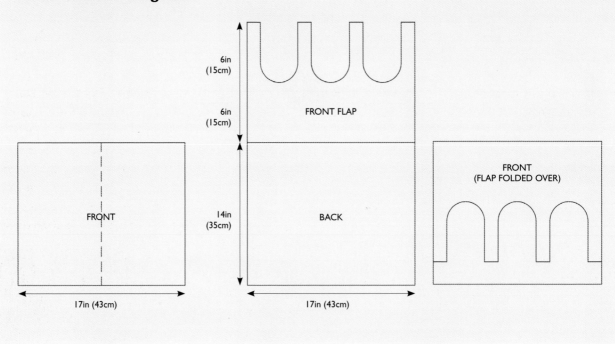

6in (15cm)

6in (15cm)

FRONT FLAP

14in (35cm)

BACK

FRONT

FRONT (FLAP FOLDED OVER)

17in (43cm)

17in (43cm)

Back and front flap

1 Ensure that the garment you are going to use is pure wool and with instructions for hand wash only. Machine wash the garment at 40°C (if you want a more felted effect wash it again at a higher temperature).

2 Cut out one rectangle for the front measuring 17 x 14in (43 x 36cm) (if you are using a waistcoat or cardigan, sew 2 matching pieces together with

a centre seam), and a 17 x 20in (43 x 51cm) piece for the back and front flap.

3 If possible use the neck and armhole shaping of the garment to make the four strips hanging on the bottom edge of the front of the flap (see diagram). If there is not enough fabric in one piece to do this, cut a rectangle measuring 17 x 14in (43 x 36cm) for the back and a separate piece of

fabric for the flap measuring 17 x 6in (43 x 15cm) plus 4 strips of fabric each measuring approximately 6in (15cm) to attach the embellishment to.

4 Place the front and back right sides together; fasten the two side seams and base seam using backstitch with the needle and thread. If the flap is a separate piece of fabric, attach this to the top of the back with a backstitch seam.

Long knitted embellishments
(make 4)

Using 4mm needles and Noro Kureyon cast on 40 sts.

Row 1: Knit.
Row 2: Purl.
Row 3: Inc 1 in every st by knitting into the front and back of st to end of row (80 sts).
Row 4: Purl.
Row 5: Knit.
Row 6: Purl.
Row 7: As row 3 (160 sts).
Row 8: Purl.

Row 9: *Inc 1 in each of 1st 20 sts (40 sts).
Turn, p40, turn, cast off 40. Rejoin yarn to remaining sts on left-hand needle and repeat from * 8 times.

Flower-shaped embellishments
(make 2)

Using 4mm needles and Noro Kureyon cast on 40 sts.
Work rows 1–8 as for the long embellishments.
Cast off.

Making up

Sew in the ends on the embellishments. Let them curl naturally, twisting them so that the knit and purl sides alternate. Fasten the 4 long strands to the 4 strips hanging down at the front of the bag. Make the other 2 strands into flower shapes by twisting and sewing at the base. These can be used to cover the centre seam of the bag if you have had to join two pieces of a cardigan or waistcoat, or place on the pockets. Fasten the large press studs to the inside of the flap and the small press studs to the inside of the pockets.

A bold and bright laptop cozy with a colourful appliqué design on the front panel and a sturdy lining for added protection. This spacious bag has plenty of room for paperwork and accessories.

Stars and stripes

Materials

22 x 16in (56 x 40.5cm) piece of patterned fabric x 2
18 x 3in (45.5 x 8cm) piece of patterned fabric x 2
10 x 8in (25.5 x 20.5cm) piece of star-patterned fabric
17 x 1½in (43 x 4cm) felt strips x 6
22 x 16in (56 x 40.5cm) piece of lining fabric x 2
18 x 3in (45.5 x 8cm) piece of lining fabric x 2

Finished size

13½ x 18 x 3¾in (34 x 46 x 9.5cm)

Front

1 Fold over, press and stitch a ½in (1.5cm) hem along each edge of the starry fabric, with mitred corners.

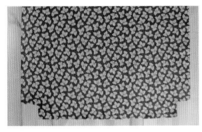

2 Cut out a 2 x 2in (5 x 5cm) square from the left and right bottom corner of one of the large pieces of patterned fabric and lay face up.

3 Pin the stripes in place with the first stripe ¾in (2cm) from the top of the fabric and the remaining 5 stripes having a 1in (2.5cm) gap between each one. The bottom stripe should come to

approximately 1in (2.5cm) above the indentations at the bottom of the fabric. Using matching thread and satin stitch, stitch the stripes in place. Then stitch the rectangle of starry fabric in the top left-hand corner on top of the first three stripes (see completed image).

Back

4 Cut out two indentations from the second large piece of patterned fabric as in step 2 and lay this right sides together on top of the appliquéd fabric. Pin and stitch the base seam, then press flat. Pin and stitch the two side seams and press flat.

5 Flatten out the base and pin and stitch across the two open gaps from the indentations.

6 Turn the bag right side out, pushing out the corners with a pencil or knitting needle.

Lining

7 Take the two pieces of lining fabric and cut and stitch in exactly the same way as above with right sides together, but do not turn right side out.

Handles (make 2 alike)

8 Place the strip of patterned fabric and strip of lining fabric right sides together and hem three edges, leaving one short edge open. Turn right side out, pushing out the corners with a pencil or knitting needle.

Finishing off

Turn a ¾in (2cm) hem down all around the top of the lining and then pin and press. Place the handle ends 4½in (11cm) in from each side seam and pin in place. Work 2 rows of stitching over each handle end and then stitch the hem for the lining in place, stitching over the handle ends once more for extra strength. Now place the lining inside the outer bag. Turn in a ¾in (2cm) hem all around the top of the outer fabric and sew the lining in place to the top edge of the bag (see page 140).

A stylish, durable cotton iPad cozy in classic cables. This simple and timeless design is a good introduction to cable knitting. It has an optional strap and is finished with a crisp crochet edging.

Classic cables

Materials

Rowan Denim 100% cotton (102yd/93m per 50g ball)

3 x 50g balls of Ecru

A pair of 4mm (UK8:US6) knitting needles

3.5mm (UK9:US/E4) crochet hook

Cable needle

1 large toggle

Finished size

Approx. 8¾ x 10¼ x ¾in (22 x 26 x 2cm) after washing

Note

Yarn amounts given are based on average requirements and are approximate.

Tension

20 sts and 28 rows to 4in (10cm) over moss stitch using 4mm needles before washing.

20 sts and 32 rows to 4in (10cm) over moss stitch using 4mm needles after washing.

Note

If substituting with a DK cotton cast on the same amount of stitches as stated in the pattern but cast off when work measures 10¼in (26cm). It is not necessary to wash a standard DK cotton before making up.

Special abbreviations

C6B = slip next 3 sts onto a cable needle at the back of work, k3 from the left-hand needle, then k3 from the cable needle.

Front

Using 4mm needles cast on 51 sts.
Row 1: K1, * p1, k1, rep from * to end.
This row sets moss stitch.
Work 4 rows more in moss stitch.
Next row: Patt 11 (m1, patt 2, m1, patt 7) 4 times, patt 4 (59 sts).
Work cable pattern as follows:
Row 1 (RS): Moss 5, * p5, k6, rep from * to last 10 sts, p5, moss 5.
Row 2: Moss 5, * k5, p6, rep from * to last 10 sts, k5, moss 5.
Rows 3 & 4: Repeat rows 1 and 2.
Row 5: Moss 5 * p5, C6B, rep from * to last 10 sts, p5, moss 5.
Row 6: Work as row 2.
Rows 7–8: Repeat rows 1 and 2.

These 8 rows form the pattern.
Work the 8-row pattern-repeat 9 times, then work rows 1–3 once more.
Next row: Keeping moss st patt correct at ends, continue in moss st as follows: Patt 10 * patt2tog, patt 2, patt2tog, patt 5, rep from * to last 5 sts, patt 5 (51 sts).
Work 5 more rows in moss st.
Cast off in moss st.

Back

Using 4mm needles cast on 51 sts.
Work in moss st as set on front until back measures the same as front.
Cast off in moss st.

Side panels
(make 2)

Using 4mm needles cast on 6 sts.
Row 1: (K1, p1) 3 times.
Row 2: (P1, k1) 3 times.
These 2 rows set moss stitch.
Work in moss st until piece measures the same as the side edge of the front and back.
Cast off in moss st.

Base

Using 4mm needles cast on 60 sts.
Work 6 rows in moss st as set on
side panels.
Cast off.

Strap (optional)

Using 4mm needles cast on 6 sts.
Work in moss st as set on side panels
until strap measures 26in (66cm).
Cast off.

Button loop

Using a 3.5mm crochet hook, crochet
a chain that measures 8in (20cm).

Making up

Sew in loose ends and wash all the
pieces according to instructions on
the ball band. Gently stretch the pieces
into shape when dry.

Stitch the two side panels on to each
end of the base to form one long strip.
With wrong sides together pin the first
side panel down the side edge of the
front (from point A to B), pin the base
along the cast-on edge of the front
piece (point B to C) and pin the
second side panel up the other side
edge of the front piece (point C to D).
Using a 3.5mm crochet hook and
starting at point A with right side facing,
crochet the two pieces together by

working a double crochet stitch through
both pieces of knitting. Continue all the
way round, working an extra chain
stitch at each of the two corners
(points B and C). Attach the back panel
in the same way. Sew in any loose ends.

Attach the strap by stitching each end
inside the side panels. Fold the button
loop in half and attach the two ends
inside the middle of the back panel.
Attach the toggle to the middle of the
front panel to correspond with the loop.

Making-up diagram

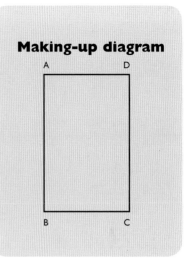

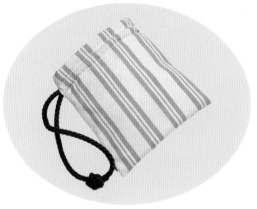

This handy drawstring bag can be used to house all your cables in one place. No longer will you be hunting for your phone charger! Simple, stylish and lined with padded fabric, this bag is also great to take on your travels.

Neat 'n' tidy

Materials

10 x 19in (25 x 48cm) piece of medium-weight fabric

10 x 19in (25 x 48cm) piece of padded lining fabric

1yd (1m) of ³⁄₁₆ or ¼in (5 or 6mm) piping cord

Finished size

9 x 10in (23 x 25cm)

Bag

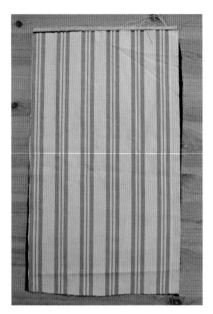

1 Take the piece of medium-weight fabric and the piece of lining fabric and place right sides together. Stitch along one long edge.

2 Open out the fabric and press the seam flat.

3 Fold the joined pieces in half with the right sides together and the seam running horizontally across the middle.

4 Place two pins on the outer fabric, one ¾in (2cm) down from the central seam and the second pin 1in (2.5cm) below the first pin. (You are going to leave this gap un-stitched.)

28

5 Baste or pin along all three edges, leaving an opening of 2½in (6cm) in the short end of the lining fabric (so that you can turn the bag right side out). Stitch all three seams, remembering to leave the two openings un-stitched.

6 Turn the bag right side out, gently pushing all the corners out with a pencil or knitting needle.

7 Hand sew the opening in the lining fabric (see page 140). Push the lining fabric down inside the outer fabric and press the top seam. Overstitch (see page 140) each side of the opening for the cord to give it extra strength.

8 Work 1 row of stitching all the way around the top of the bag ¾in (2cm) down from the top edge. Work another row of stitching all the way around 1in (2.5cm) below the first row.

9 Attach a safety pin to one end of the cord, then feed this through the pocket until it comes out at the other end.

Finishing off
Fasten the two ends of the cord with a knot.

This supersoft armband is knitted in a machine-washable wool blend for extra elasticity and has a snug pocket to slip your iPod into for easy listening while you are exercising.

Keep on running

Materials

Debbie Bliss Cashmerino Aran (98yd/90m per 50g ball)

1 x 50g ball of charcoal (A)

1 x 50g ball of red (B)

A pair of 4.5mm (UK7:US7) needles

4.5mm (UK7:US7) short circular needle

Finished size

Approx. 12½ x 6½in (32 x 17cm) when stretched

Note

Yarn amounts given are based on average requirements and are approximate.

Tension

18 sts and 24 rows to 4in (10cm) measured over stocking stitch using 4.5mm needles.

Note

This is designed to fit a bare upper arm: to enlarge the size, increase the amount of stitches in blocks of 4.

Pocket back

Using yarn A and straight needles cast on 10 sts.

Row 1 (RS): * K2, p2, rep from * to last 2 sts, k2.

Row 2: * P2, k2, rep from * to last 2 sts, p2.

Repeat these 2 rows until work measures 4in (10cm) ending on a WS row; leave sts on a spare needle.

Armband

Using yarn A and the circular needle cast on 44 sts.

Round 1: * K2, p2, rep from * to end of round.

This round sets 2x2 rib.

Work in 2x2 rib in the round, changing colours as follows:

Work 4 rows in A

Work 2 rows in B.

Continue until work measures 5in (13cm).

Attach pocket back

At the beginning of the next round cast off 10 sts and break yarn. Rejoin yarn to the sts on the spare needle, work in 2x2 rib across these 10 sts and continue in the round keeping rib pattern and stripe pattern correct. Continue until work measures 6½in (17cm).

Cast off in rib.

Making up

Sew pocket back in place and sew in ends.

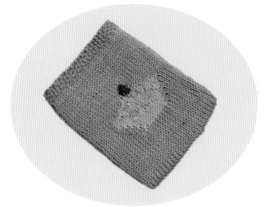

A super cute cozy for a portable hard drive or compact camera knitted in mercerised cotton. The sweet cupcake design uses the intarsia method of knitting with colour and a small amount of beading.

Cupcake

Materials

Rowan Cotton Glace 100% cotton
(126yd/115m per 50g ball)
1 x 50g ball of Blue (A)
Oddments of Gold (B), Pink (C) and Red (D)
A pair each of 3mm (UK11:US2–3) and 3.25mm
(UK10:US3) needles
7 glass beads (size 6/0)

Finished size

4¼ x 5½in (13.5 x 12.75cm)

Tension

23 sts and 32 rows to 4in (10cm) over stocking stitch using 3.25mm needles.

Pattern note

MB – make bobble by knitting into the front, back and front again of the next st, turn, knit into each st twice (6 sts), turn, k6, turn, k3tog (twice), turn, k3tog.

Front and back

Using 3mm needles and shade A cast on 31 sts.

Row 1 (RS): * K1, p1, rep from * to last st, k1.

This row forms the moss stitch edging; repeat 3 more times.

Change to 3.25mm needles, beg with a K row continue in st st until work measures 5½in (12.75cm), ending with a WS row.

Make fold line

Next row: Purl.

Next row: Purl.

Beg with a K row, continue in st st for 12 rows.

Thread yarn C with the 7 beads (see page 151). Working from the chart in st st and using the intarsia technique (see page 149), changing the colours as indicated and placing the beads in the positions shown in the chart, continue until the chart has been completed.

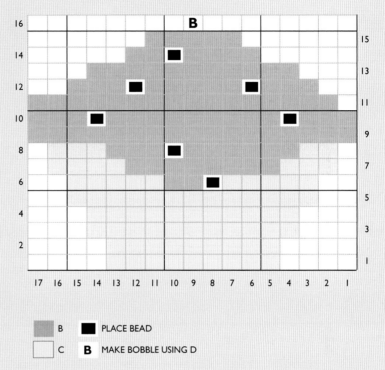

Cupcake chart *17 sts x 16 rows*
Each square = 1 st and 1 row

	B
	B PLACE BEAD
	C	B MAKE BOBBLE USING D

Continue in yarn A until front matches back up to the moss st edging. Change to 3mm needles and work 4 rows in moss st as before.
Cast off.

Making up

Sew in the loose ends, fold in half at the fold line and sew up the two side seams. Make a basic lining (see page 140) to fit into the outer cozy and sew in place just under the moss stitch edging.

With its 70s' vibe, this fun and colourful crochet cozy for a video camera is sure to get you noticed! It is made from granny squares in a soft double-knit cotton and is double lined to protect your video camera from damage.

Granny chic

Materials

Rowan Handknit Cotton (93yd/85m per 50g ball)
1 x 50g ball each of Ecru (A), Pink (B), Green (C), Royal (D), Purple (E), Red (F), Orange (G) and Turquoise (H)
4mm (UK8:USG6) crochet hook
4 buttons
13 x 9in (33 x 23cm) piece of quilted fabric
13 x 9in (33 x 23cm) piece of lining fabric
5 x 5in (12 x 12cm) piece of quilted fabric x 2
5 x 5in (12 x 12cm) piece of lining fabric x 2

8 x 4in (20 x 10cm) piece of quilted fabric
8 x 4in (20 x 10cm) piece of lining fabric

Finished size

Approx. 8 x 4 x 4in (20 x 10 x 10cm)

Note

Yarn amounts given are based on average requirements and are approximate.

Tension

One square measures 4 × 4in
(10 × 10cm) using 4mm crochet hook.

Squares

Square 1

Using yarn A, ch 4. Make a ring with a
sl st by inserting the hook into the last
chain from the hook and drawing the
yarn through.

Round 1: Using A, chain 5, *work 3
tr(s) into ring, ch 2. Repeat from *
twice more, work 2 tr(s) into ring, join
with a sl st to the 3rd ch.
Cut yarn.

Round 2: Using yarn B, sl st into the
next space, ch 5, work 3 tr(s) into
same space, *ch 1, work 3 tr(s) in next
space, ch 2, work 3 tr(s) in same space.
Repeat from * twice more, ch 1, work
2 tr(s). Join with a sl st to the 3rd ch.
Cut yarn.

Round 3: Using yarn C, sl st into the
next space, ch 5, work 3 tr(s) into
the same space, *ch 1, work 3 tr(s)
into the next space, ch 1, work 3
tr(s) into the next space, ch 2, work
3 tr(s) into the same space. Repeat
from * twice more, ch 1, work 3 tr(s)
into next space, ch 1, work 2 tr(s) into
same space as the 5 ch at the start of
round. Join with a sl st to the 3rd ch.
Cut yarn.

Round 4: Using yarn D, sl st into the
next sp, ch 5, work 3 tr(s) into the
same sp, * ch 1, work 3 tr(s) into the
next sp, ch 1, work 3 tr(s) into next sp,
ch 1, work 3 tr(s) into next sp, ch 2,
work 3 tr(s) into same space. Repeat
from * twice more, ch 1, work 3 tr(s)
into next space, ch 1, work 3 tr(s) into
next space, ch 1, work 2 tr(s) into
same space as the 5 ch at the start of
round. Join with a sl st to the 3rd ch.
Cut yarn.

Remaining squares

Make a further 9 squares using one
colour for each round and using the
full range of colours at random as
shown in the image.

Making up

Sew in any loose ends. Place 6 squares together in three rows of 2 squares and join with a flat seam. Take 2 more squares and sew 1 to each end of the middle row of 2 squares, then join the side edges of each of these squares to the side edge of each of the end squares in the top and bottom row so that you have a rectangular box (see diagram). Sew the final two squares together and join to one long edge of the box to form a lid. Using shade B, work 2 rows of double crochet along the three edges of the lid, working 3 double crochet into each of the two corners at the front of the lid.

Button loops

Place the crochet hook in the centre of the side edge of the lid and using shade B, work a chain of 12 sts, then fasten off. Work another three loops in the same way evenly around the lid. Sew the buttons onto the main part to correspond with the loops.

Lining
Main part

Place the larger rectangular pieces of quilted fabric and lining fabric right sides together and stitch all the way round leaving an opening of 3in (8cm) on one of the short edges. Turn the fabric right side out and neatly slipstitch the opening.

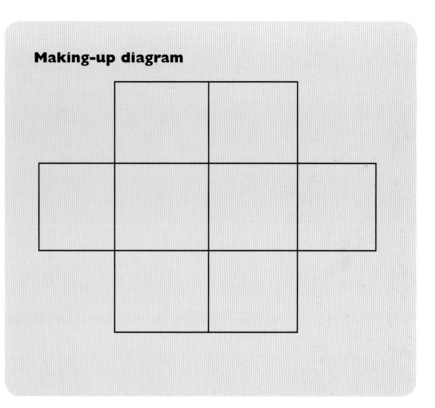

Making-up diagram

Place one square piece of quilted fabric and one square piece of lining fabric right sides together and stitch leaving an opening of 2in (5cm) on one edge. Turn right side out and slipstitch the opening. Repeat with the remaining two pieces. These are the two end panels for the box. Place the lining inside the crochet box and neatly slipstitch all around the top edges. Now fold the larger piece of lining into three and neatly stitch each end piece in place down the long side of the base and sides (see diagram).

Lid

Place the smaller rectangular pieces of quilted fabric and lining fabric right sides together and stitch all the way round leaving an opening of 3in (8cm) on one of the short edges. Turn the fabric right side out and neatly slip stitch the opening. Place it on the inside of the lid and slipstitch in place.

A soft, snug, simple cozy with an optional padded lining to protect your mobile phone. It is knitted in a variegated sock yarn and has a ribbed cuff at the top with a shaped toe piece. A great little gift for a friend!

Snug sock

Materials
Crystal Palace Mini Mochi (197yd/180m per 50g ball)
1 x 50g ball of 116 Feldspar
A pair of 2.25mm (UK13:US1) needles

Finished size
4 x 5in (10 x 12.5cm) with cuff turned down

Tension

32 sts and 44 rows to 4in (10cm) over stocking stitch using 2.25mm needles.

Front and back
(make 2 alike)

Cast on 34 sts.

Row 1 (RS): * K2, p2, rep from * to last 2 sts, k2.

Row 2: * P2, k2, rep from * to last 2 sts, p2.

Work in 2x2 rib as above for a further 16 rows.

Beg with a K row, continue in st st until work measures 5½in (12.75cm) from cast on edge, ending with a WS row.

Shape toe

Next row (RS): K1, sl 1, k1, psso, work to last 3 sts, k2tog, k1 (32sts).

Next and every foll alt row: Purl. Repeat these two rows until 22 sts rem.

Next row: K1, k2tog to end of row, k1. (12 sts).

Next row: Purl.

Cast off.

Making up

Place the two pieces right sides together, stitch the side seams and base. Turn right side out. Line with a basic lining (see page 140), if wanted, up to the start of the ribbing. Turn the ribbing down to form a cuff.

This funky fabric design will keep your iPod safe and super stylish! The lined cozy is padded for extra protection and has a handy pocket for storing the earphones.

All that jazz

Materials

7 x 3½in (18 x 9cm) piece of medium-weight fabric co-ordinating with main fabric (fabric A)
7 x 6in (18 x 15cm) light-weight sew-in interfacing
7 x 6in (18 x 15cm) piece of medium-weight cotton or linen fabric x 2 (fabrics B and C)
Button fastening
Small press stud

Finished size

Approx. 5¼ x 3¼in (13.5 x 8cm)

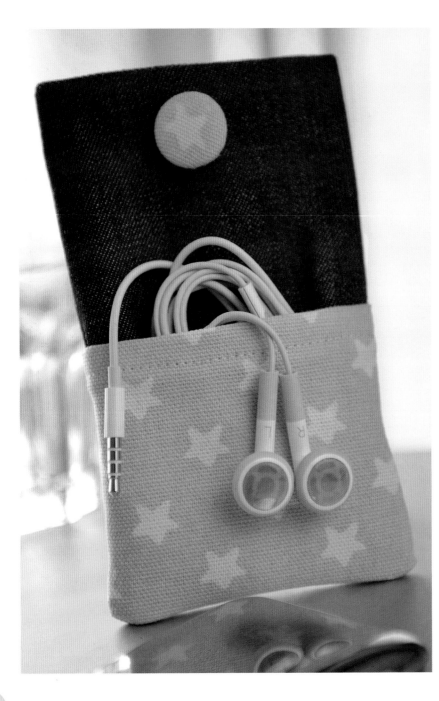

Pocket

1 Fold over a ¾in (2cm) hem down one long side of the pocket (fabric A) and stitch. Press.

Front and back

2 Lay the interface lining down. On top of this lay the cozy fabric (fabric B) right side up and on top of this lay the lining fabric (fabric C) right side down. Pin the 3 layers together across one of the short edges and stitch with a ¾in (2cm) allowance.

3 Open out with the lining and interfacing above the seam and the outer cozy fabric below the seam. Press the seam flat.

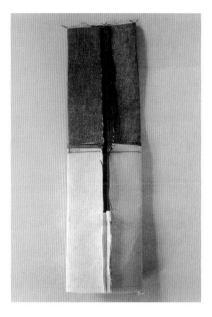

4 Lay the pocket right side up onto the bottom half of the cozy fabric and pin in place.

5 Fold the joined pieces in half lengthwise (right sides together) with the seam running horizontally across the middle and stitch down the long edge. Press the seam open, ensuring it is now in the centre of the tube.

6 Stitch across the bottom of the tube.

7 Turn the tube right side out through the hole in the lining. Stitch the hem of the lining by turning in the raw edges.

Finishing off

Push the lining into the cozy, pushing out the corners with a pencil or knitting needle, and press the whole piece. Place the button on the outside of the cozy (see photograph on facing page for position) and sew the press stud inside the cozy to correspond with the button.

This smart crochet cozy will store a Kindle or iPad. It is worked in treble crochet, alternating stripes of a solid shade with a gorgeous multicoloured yarn, and is fastened with Velcro.

Multi-toned

Materials

2 x 50g balls of Noro Kureyon (109yd/100m per 50g ball)
(A) shade 219
1 x 50g ball of Debbie Bliss Rialto Aran (87yd/80m per 50g)
(B) shade 28 Purple
4.5mm (UK7:US7) crochet hook
16 x 10in (40 x 25cm) padded lining fabric
10in (25cm) Velcro

Finished size

10 x 8in plus 4in flap (25 x 20cm plus 10cm)

Note

Yarn amounts given are based on average requirements and are approximate.

Tension

7 clusters and 7 rows to 4in (10cm) using 4.5mm crochet hook.

Front, back and flap
(one piece)

Using B chain 39. Working from pattern below change the colours as follows:
5 rows of B
10 rows of A.

Row 1: Work 2 tr into 4th ch from hook, leave last st of each tr on hook, then yo hook and yarn through all 3 sts, *ch 1, skip 1 ch, 3 tr into next ch, leave last st of each tr on hook, then yo hook and yarn through all 3 sts, repeat from * to end of row, ch 5, turn.

Row 2: Work 3 tr in 5-chain loop, *ch 1, skip 1 ch, 3 tr into next ch, leave last st of each tr on hook, then yo hook and yarn through all 3 sts, repeat from * to end of row, ch 5, turn.

Repeat row 2, changing colours as above, until work measures approx 20in (51cm), ending with a 5th row using B.

Lining

The lining fabric should be the same width as the crocheted piece and 4in (10cm) shorter. Stitch a ½in (1.5cm) seam around all 4 sides. With wrong sides together lay the lining fabric on the crochet fabric (leaving the top 4in/10cm of the crochet fabric unlined for the flap) and neatly sew into place (see page 141). With the lining fabric on the outside make a fold halfway up the lining fabric. Sew up the two side seams of the crochet fabric. Turn right side out.

Making up

Fasten a piece of Velcro along the inside of the flap and the corresponding piece of Velcro along the front of the cozy.

A mini stitched cozy that can be used to tidy up gadget paraphernalia such as earphones and spare batteries. The easy design is simple enough for a child to make and is embellished with handmade ceramic buttons.

Autumnal fall

Materials

3 x 11in (8 x 28cm) piece of rust wool felt
5 x 5½in (12 x 12.75cm) piece of navy wool felt x 2
Pinking shears
2 leaf buttons

Finished size

5 x 5½in (12 x 12.75cm)

Front and back

1 Cut a 2in (5cm) strip lengthwise from the rust felt. From this piece of felt, cut a basic leaf shape 3in (8cm) long and 2in (5cm) wide at the widest part, using the pinking shears, and two small strips measuring ¼in (0.5cm) × 2in (5cm) using ordinary scissors.

2 Sew the leaf onto one piece of the navy felt at an angle as shown in the image.

3 Take one of the small strips of felt and using running stitch up one long edge, gather the felt into a flower bud shape. Fasten off the thread and sew on to the top of the leaf. Repeat with the other strip of fabric and position as shown in the photograph.

4 Place the two rectangles of navy felt together, wrong sides together, pin and stitch leaving a ½in (1.5cm) hem. Trim round all four edges with the pinking shears.

Lining

5 Make a basic padded lining (see page 140), insert in the cozy and sew along the top edge neatly by hand (see page 141).

Finishing off

Take the remaining strip of rust felt that measures 1 × 11in (2.5 × 28cm). Trim all around it with the pinking shears. Fasten each end to the front and back top corner of the cozy with a button.

A classic Fair Isle design makes a contemporary cosy for a mobile phone, iPod or compact camera. It is knitted using the Fair Isle method of weaving the yarns at the back of the work and then lined with a basic lining.

Fair Isle

Materials

Rowan Pure Wool 4ply 100% wool (approx. 175yd/160m per 50g ball)

1 x 50g ball of Blue (A)

Oddments of Rust (B), Pale grey (C), Cream (D), Lilac (E) and Dark Green (F)

A pair each of 3mm (UK11:US2–3) and 3.25mm (UK10:US3) needles

1 button

10 x 3¾in (25.5 x 9.5cm) piece of lining fabric

Finished size

Approx. 4¾ x 4¼in (12.5 x 11cm)

Note

Yarn amounts given are based on average requirements and are approximate.

Make buttonhole

Next row: (K1, p1) 6 times, k1, yfwd, k2tog, pattern to end of row.
Next row: Pattern to end of row.
Work 2 more rows in moss st.
Cast off.

Making up

Sew in all the loose ends. Place the two pieces right sides together and sew the two side edges and bottom seam using back stitch. Turn right side out so that the right side is now on the outside. Fold over the flap and sew the button on the front to correspond with the buttonhole. Make and insert a basic lining (see page 140).

Tension

29 sts and 36 rows to 4in (10cm) over fair-isle using 3.25mm needles.

Front

*Using 3.25mm needles and A cast on 31 sts.
Row 1 (WS): Purl.
Next row: Beg with a knit row and continue in st st, working pattern from the chart (read from right to left on the knit rows and from left to right on the purl rows).
After row 28 of the chart has been worked repeat rows 1–11.
Next row (WS): Purl.
Change to 3mm needles and continue as follows:

Next row (RS): K1, (p1, k1) to end.
This row sets moss stitch.**
Work 3 rows more in moss st.
Cast off.

Back

Work as Front from * to **.
Continue in moss st for a further 14 rows.

Fair Isle chart *31 sts x 28 rows*
Each square = 1 st and 1 row

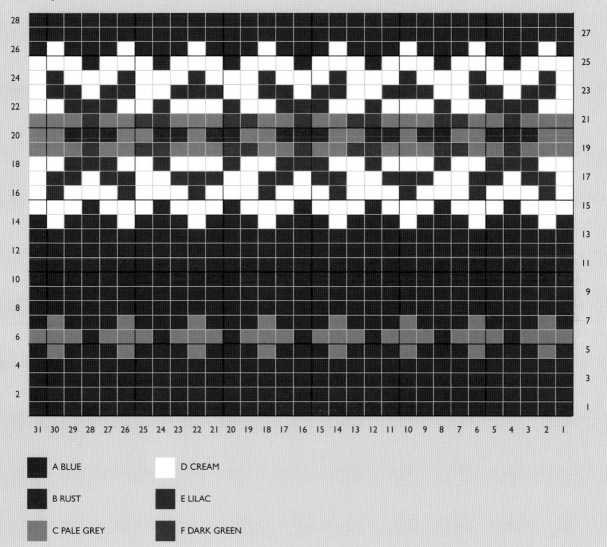

A BLUE
B RUST
C PALE GREY
D CREAM
E LILAC
F DARK GREEN

This cute felted cozy looks great hung on a hook and is the perfect size to store the cables that accompany your gadgets. It's embellished with geometric shapes and then felted in the washing machine to create a sturdy little bag.

Patches

Materials

Jamieson & Smith 2ply Jumper Weight yarn 100% wool
(126yd/115m per 25g ball)
2 × 25g balls (used double) of Ochre (A)
Small quantities of Rust (B), Lovat Green (C)
and Dark Green (D)
A pair each of 2.75mm (UK12:US2) and 4mm
(UK8:US6) needles
2 buttons
14 × 6in (36 × 15cm) piece of lining fabric
2 press studs

Size

7½ × 8in (19 × 20cm) before washing
Approx. 5½ × 6½in (14 × 17cm) after washing

Note

Yarn amounts given are based on average requirements and are approximate.

Tension
(before washing)
19 sts and 29 rows to 4in (10cm) over stocking stitch using yarn double and 4mm needles.

30 sts and 38 rows to 4in (10cm) over stocking stitch using yarn single and 2.75mm needles.

Front and back
(1 piece)
Using 2 strands of A and 4mm needles cast on 36 sts and work in g-st for 4 rows.
Beg with a K row, continue in st st until work measures 8in (20cm), ending on a RS row.

Make fold line
Next row: Knit.
Next row: Knit.
Next row: Purl.
Continue in st st until work measures 7½in (19.5cm) from fold line. Work in g-st for 4 rows.
Cast off.

Strap
Using 2 strands of A and 4mm needles cast on 70 sts.
Work in g-st for 2 rows.
Next row: K4, cast off 3 sts, k to last 7 sts, cast off 3 sts, k3.
Next row: K4, cast on 3 sts, k to last

7 sts, cast on 3 sts, k4.
Work in g-st for 2 more rows.
Cast off.

Embellishments
Squares (make 2 the same)
*Using 2.25mm needles and one strand of B cast on 12 sts.
Beg with a K row, work in st st for 18 rows. Cast off.**
Using one strand of C repeat from * to **.

Triangles (make 2 the same)
Using 2.25mm needles and one strand of D cast on 15 sts.
Beg with a K row, working in st st shape as follows:
Work 2 rows.
Row 3: K1, k2tog, k to last 3 sts k2tog, k1 (13 sts).

Row 4: Purl.
Repeat last 2 rows until 5 sts remain.
Next row: K1, k3tog, k1 (3 sts).
Next row: Purl.
Next row: K3tog.
Fasten off.

Making up
Fasten the embellishments by over-sewing two corners on each so that the edges curl naturally (see completed image). Fold the cozy in half at the fold line and join the side seams with mattress stitch. Sew a button onto the top right-hand corner of the front and the same for the back and attach the strap. Machine wash at 40°C. Stretch into shape while damp. Make a basic lining (see page 140) and insert. Fasten the two press studs to the inside of the top edge.

A fabulously cozy case for a laptop, knitted in chunky cables in a tweedy yarn and lined with padded fabric. The oversized buttons complete this stylish design.

Chunky cables

Materials

Debbie Bliss Luxury Tweed Chunky (10yd/100m per 100g skein)
3 x 100g skeins of shade 09 Flame
A pair each of 5.5mm (UK5:US9) and 6.5mm (UK3:US10.5) needles
2 large buttons
¾in (21mm) press studs x 2
16 x 33in (41 x 13cm) piece of lining fabric

Finished size

16 x 14in (41 x 36cm)

Note

Yarn amounts given are based on average requirements and are approximate.

Tension

16 sts and 20 rows to 4in (10cm) worked across cable pattern B using 6.5mm needles.

Special abbreviations

C4b – cable 4 back – slip next 2 sts onto cable needle at back of work, k next 2 sts, then k2 sts from cable needle.

T3f – Twist 3 at the front by slipping next 2 sts onto cable needle at front of work, p1, then k2 from cable needle.

T3b – twist 3 at the back by slipping next st onto cable needle at back of work, k2, then p1 from cable needle.

C12b – cable 12 at the back by slipping next 6 sts onto cable needle at back of work, k6, then k6 from cable needle.

C12f – cable 12 at the front by slipping next 6 sts onto cable needle at front of work, k6, then k6 from cable needle.

Cable panel A

(12 sts)

Row 1 (RS): K12.
Row 2: P12.
Row 3: C12b.
Row 4: P12.
Rows 5 to 10: Repeat rows 1 and 2 a further 3 times.
Repeat these 10 rows.

Cable panel B

(16 sts)

Row 1 (RS): K2, p4, k4, p4, k2.
Row 2: P2, k4, p4, k4, p2.
Row 3: K2, p4, C4b, p4, k2.
Row 4: Repeat row 2.
Row 5: (T3f, p2, T3b) twice.
Row 6: K1, p2, (k2, p2) 3 times, k1.
Row 7: P1, T3f, T3b, p2, T3f, T3b, p1.
Row 8: K2, p4, k4, p4, k2.
Row 9: P2, C4b, p4, C4b, p2.
Row 10: Repeat row 8.
Row 11: P2, k4, p4, k4, p2.
Rows 12 and 13: Repeat rows 8 and 9.
Row 14: Repeat row 8.
Row 15: P1, T3b, T3f, p2, T3b, T3f, p1.
Row 16: Repeat row 6.
Row 17: (T3b, p2, T3f) twice.
Rows 18 and 19: Repeat rows 2 and 3.
Row 20: Repeat row 2.
Repeat these 20 rows.

Cable panel C

(12 sts)

Row 1 (RS): K12.
Row 2: P12.
Row 3: C12f.
Row 4: P12.
Rows 5 to 10: Repeat rows 1 and 2 3 times.
Repeat these 10 rows.

Main part

Using 5.5mm needles cast on 59 sts. Work 2 rows in g-st.

Next row (WS): K5, *m1, k6, rep from * to end of row (68 sts). Change to 6.5mm needles.

Row 1: K6, p4, k12, p4, k2, p4, k4, p4, k2, p4, k12, p4, k6 (this forms the first row of cable panels A, B and C).

Row 2: P6, k4, work row 2 of cable pattern C, k4, work row 2 of cable pattern B, k4, work row 2 of cable pattern A, k4, p6.

Row 3: K6, p4, work row 3 of cable pattern A, p4, work row 3 of cable pattern B, p4, work row 3 of cable pattern C, p4, k6.

Row 4: P6, k4, work row 4 of cable pattern C, k4, work row 4 of cable pattern B, k4, work row 4 of cable pattern A, k4, p6.

Row 5 onwards: Continue to work the stitches between the cable panels as set and repeat the cable patterns until the work measures approximately 31½–35½in (80–90cm), ending on row 20 of cable pattern B.

Next row: Using 5.5mm needles k6, *k2tog, k5, rep from * to last 6 sts, k2tog, k4. (59 sts).
Work 2 rows in g-st.
Cast off.

Making up

Fastenings

Sew the two buttons just below the cast-off edge in the centre of cable panels A and C. Fasten the tops of the press studs behind the buttons and the base of the press studs in the centre of cable panels A and C 7in (18cm) up from cast-on edge.

Lining

Pin out and block the knitting to size. Stitch a hem around all four edges of the lining fabric. Place it wrong sides together with the piece of knitting, pin in place then neatly sew around the edges by hand (see page 141). Lay the work with the lining facing down, then turn up the bottom edge to make a fold line 14in (36cm) from the bottom (right sides of knitting together). Stitch down the two side seams along the edge of the fabric lining (see page 140). Turn right side out.

An adorable cozy for a mobile phone or iPod that will appeal to kids large and small. The case is worked in double crochet and embellished with crochet patches and embroidery.

Ollie the owl

Materials

Rowan Cotton Glace (126yd/115m per 50g ball)

1 x 50g ball of pink (A)

Oddments of purple (B) and cream (C)

3mm (UK11:USC/2–D/3) crochet hook

Finished size

3 x 5in (8 x 12cm)

Note

Yarn amounts given are based on average requirements and are approximate.

Tension

18 sts and 12 rows to 4in (10cm) over double crochet using 3mm crochet hook.

Main part

Using A ch 25.

Row 1: 1 dc into 2nd ch from hook, 1 dc into each ch to end, turn.

Row 2: 1 ch (does count as a st), 1 dc into each ch to end, turn.

Row 2 sets dc fabric.

Continue as set until work measures 6¼in (16cm).

Fasten off.

Wings

(make 2)

Using B ch 6 work 9 rows in dc fabric as set on main part to make a square. Fasten off.

Eyes

(make 2)

Using C ch 4, work 9 tr in last ch from hook, join with a sl st.

Fasten off.

Making up

Fold main part in half lengthwise with right sides together, then sew the two long edges together using mattress stitch. Flatten out so that the seam runs down the middle of the back and sew along the bottom edge. Sew the wings and eyes in place as shown in the image. Using shade B, embroider a French knot (see page 141) in the centre of each eye and, using satin stitch, embroider a beak.

Ears

Make two tassels by wrapping shade B 10 times around a piece of card measuring 4in (10cm), then cut through one end of the loops. Fold in half to make a loop and pull through the top corners with a crochet hook. Pass the fringe through the loop and pull tight.

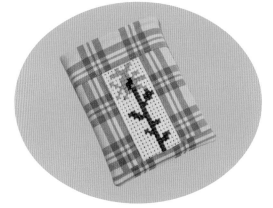

A neat little cozy for a portable hard drive that incorporates a
basic cross-stitch design of a sunflower framed by strips of fabric.
It is lined for extra protection and fastened with a press stud.

Sunflower

Materials

4 x 6in (10 x 15cm) piece of cross-stitch fabric
(7 holes per inch)
Tapestry wool or 4ply knitting yarn, small amounts of gold,
green and brown
2 x 7in (5 x 18cm) piece of fabric x 2
2 x 6in (5 x 15cm) piece of fabric x 2
6 x 7in (15 x 18cm) piece of fabric
12 x 7in (30.5 x 18cm) piece of lining fabric
Press stud

Finished size

5 x 6in (12 x 15cm)

Sunflower cross stitch

Stitch the sunflower design from the chart on to the piece of cross-stitch fabric, working the stitches as described on page 139.

Front

1 Take the 2 pieces of 2 x 7in (5 x 18cm) fabric. Fold under and press a ½in (1.5cm) hem on one long side of each piece of fabric. If the fabric is patterned, make sure that the design matches when the hemmed edges are placed together.

2 Pin each piece of fabric down the side of the embroidered motif and stitch in place.

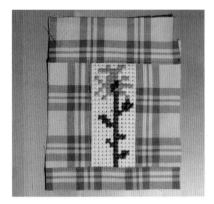

3 Repeat steps 1 and 2 with the remaining two pieces of fabric at the top and bottom of the stitched motif.

Sunflower chart
12 sts x 28 rows
Each square =
1 st and 1 row

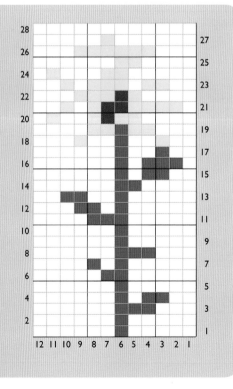

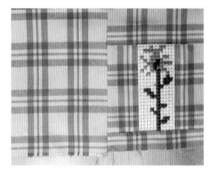

Back and lining

4 Place the piece of fabric measuring 6 x 7in (15 x 18cm) right sides together with the front. Pin and stitch a ½in (1.5cm) seam down one long edge. Press the seam flat and open out.

5 Place this right sides together with the lining fabric, pin and stitch a ½in (1.5cm) seam along the top edge, open out and press seam flat.

6 Fold the fabric in half vertically. Pin and stitch the two short edges and one long edge with a ½in (1.5cm) seam allowance and leaving a 3in (8cm) opening at the top of the lining fabric.

7 Turn right side out through the opening and hand sew the opening (see page 140).

Finishing off

Press flat and push the lining inside the outer cozy, poking out the corners with a pencil. Press gently. Centre the press stud inside the top opening and stitch on carefully to the lining fabric, making sure the stitches don't come through to the outer fabric.

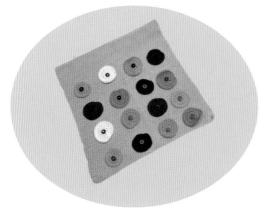

This striking crochet design will cover a computer screen and brighten up your home office. The crochet background is embellished with colourful circles, which are held in place with buttons.

Polka dot

Materials

Rowan Handknit Cotton (93yd/85m per 50g ball)
5 x 50g balls of Linen (A)
1 x 50g ball each of Red (B), Green (C), Gold (D), Navy (E), Turquoise (F), White (G) and Plum (H)
4mm (UK8:USG/6) crochet hook
16 buttons

Finished size

18 x 20in (46 x 51cm) to fit a 17/18in (43/46cm) screen

Note

Yarn amounts given are based on average requirements and are approximate.

Tension

16 sts and 10 rows to 4in (10cm) over pattern using 4mm crochet hook.

Main part

Using shade A ch 88 sts.

Row 1: Work 1 htr in 3rd chain from hook and continue to the end of the row working htr in every st (86 sts), ch 2, turn.

Repeat this row until work measures 20in (51cm).

Fasten off.

Polka dots

Using one of the contrast shades (see quantities below) ch 5, join round with sl st into 1st ch.

Round 1: Work 9 tr in last chain from hook.

Round 2: Work 2 tr in each st (18 sts).

Rounds 3 and 4: Repeat round 2 (72 sts).

Fasten off.

Colours for polka dots

B x 2 circles

C x 3 circles

D x 3 circles

E x 1 circle

F x 3 circles

G x 2 circles

H x 2 circles

Making up

Sew in any loose ends on main part and polka dots. Make a 2in (5cm) hem across the top short edge of the main part. Place the polka dots in even stripes of 4 x 4 and attach with a button in the centre of each. Hook the hemmed edge over the back of the computer screen and weigh down with a piece of wood or dowel if needed.

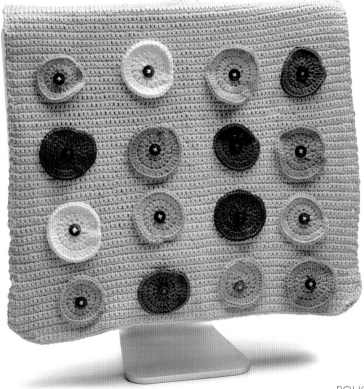

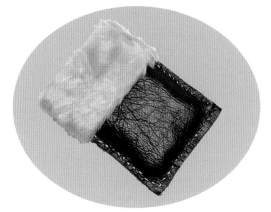

A luxurious, fur-lined cozy to keep your mobile phone snug.
The hand-stitched leather is lined with a fur fabric, but for the
ultimate in luxury you could use real sheepskin.

Biggles

Materials

4¼ x 5in (12 x 13cm) piece of leather or faux leather x 2
4¼ x 5in (12 x 13cm) piece of fur fabric x 2
4 x 11in (10 x 28cm) piece of fur fabric
Heavy-duty sewing needle or needle for sewing leather
Extra-strong sewing thread or embroidery thread

Finished size

4¼ x 6in (12 x 15cm)

Front and back

1 Cut the leather and fur fabric to the measurements above, ensuring that the leather pieces have perfectly straight edges.

2 Place the two pieces of leather fabric wrong sides together and using a heavy-duty needle and strong thread, sew by hand in running stitch down one long side, across the base and up the other long side.

Lining

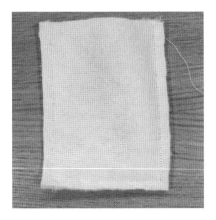

3 Place the two pieces of fur fabric right sides together. Stitch up the two long sides and across one short end.

4 Place the fur lining inside the leather pouch using a pencil or knitting needle to push out the corners.

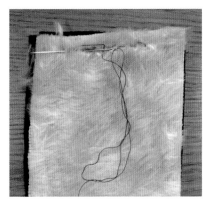

5 Using a heavy-duty needle (for denim and thicker fabrics), stitch the fur lining to the leather just inside the top edge. This does not need to go along the full length of the opening – it is just to keep the lining in place.

Cuff

6 To check the size of the cuff, wrap the long strip of fur fabric around the top of the leather pouch (wrong side facing the leather) and pin the two short ends together.

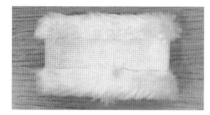

7 Take the cuff off and stitch the seam where it is pinned. Turn over a hem of ¾in (2cm) at the top and bottom of the cuff and stitch into place on the wrong side.

Finishing off

Turn right side out. Place the cuff over the top of the leather pouch so that the opening of the pouch is approximately ¾in (2cm) below the top of the cuff, then stitch the fur lining to the inside of the cuff.

This handy cozy will store three remote controls for the TV, DVD and stereo, and just tucks between the cushion and arm of a sofa or armchair. The size can easily be increased to take more controls if needed.

Zapper

Materials

22 x 11in (56 x 28cm) piece of medium-weight fabric
12½ x 32in (4.75 x 81cm) piece of medium-weight fabric x 2

Finished size

30 x 11½in (76 x 29cm)

Note

If you want to create storage for more controls, increase the width of the small piece of fabric by 7in (18cm) per pocket and the larger pieces of fabric by 3½in (9cm) per pocket.

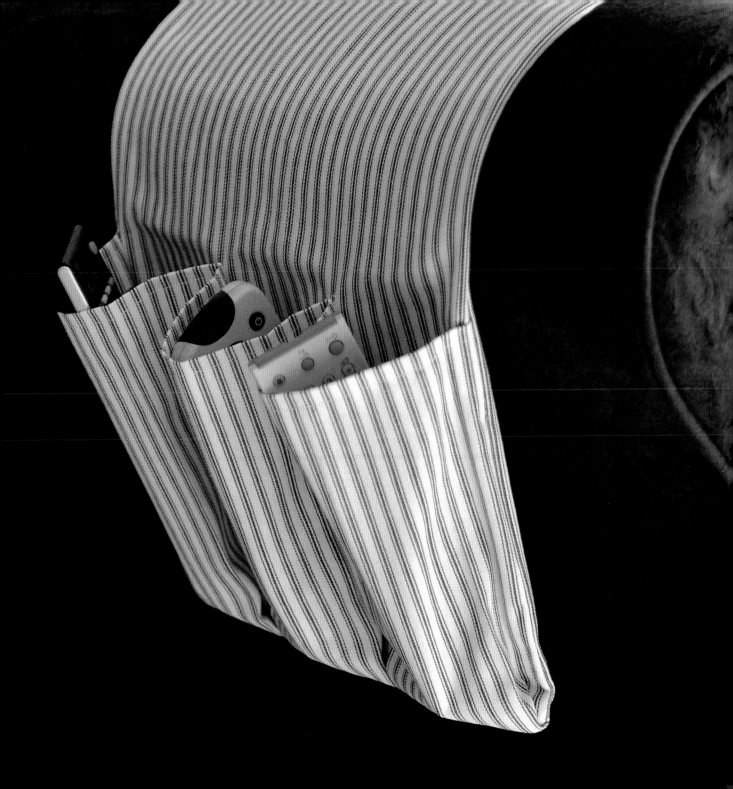

Pockets

1 Turn down a 1in (2.5cm) hem along both long edges of the small piece of fabric. Pin, press and stitch in place.

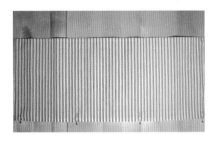

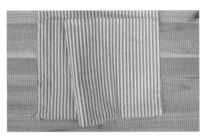

2 With the right side of fabric facing, place a pin ½in (1.5cm) in from the raw edge, followed by three more pins placed at 7in (18cm) intervals.

3 Place this piece of fabric on top of one of the larger pieces of fabric, both with right sides facing up and the bottom long edge of the small piece of fabric flush (there will be a concertina of fabric in the centre) with the bottom short edge of the large piece of fabric.

4 Pin both pieces of fabric together with the first pin ½in (1cm) in from the side edge and repeat with a second pin at the top of the small piece of fabric.

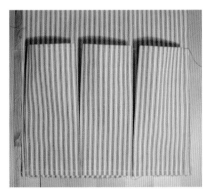

5 Measure 3½in (9cm) from the first pin on the base fabric, concertina the top fabric so that the second pin meets this point and pin in place top and bottom. Repeat this pleating action with the remaining two pins so that you have three pockets.

6 Stitch a straight seam vertically between each set of two pins to make the three pockets. Fold the fabric into box pleats and press, then stitch along the bottom edge through the pleats and base fabric.

Backing

7 Push the two outer pockets towards the middle of the fabric and pin to stop them getting caught in the backing seam.

8 Place the remaining piece of fabric right side down onto the piece with the pockets. Pin all 4 seams with a ½in (1.5cm) seam allowance and leaving a 4in (10cm) opening at the top to turn it right side out.

Finishing off

Stitch all the seams and press them flat. Turn right side out through the gap at the top and sew the opening by hand (see page 140). Press the pockets and seams.

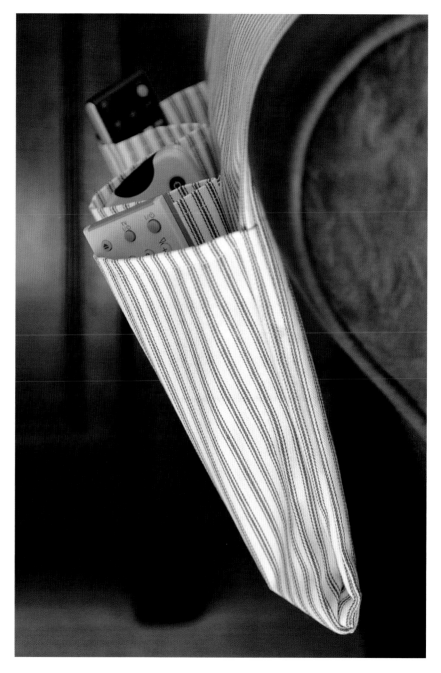

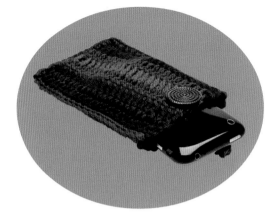

This simple introduction to crochet is worked in treble crochet, changing the colours every few rows. The soft cotton yarn is lined with felt and fastened with a button to make an iPhone, compact camera or iPod cozy.

Treble clef

Materials

Rowan Handknit Cotton (93yd/85m per 50g ball)
Small amounts of Chocolate (A), Rust (B) and Olive (C)
4mm (UK8:USG/6) crochet hook
1 button
3½ x 11in (9 x 28cm) piece of felt

Finished size

3½ x 5½in (9 x 14cm)

Note

Yarn amounts given are based on average requirements and are approximate.

Front and back
(both the same)

Using A ch 26

Row 1: work 1 treble into 4th chain from hook, work 1 tr into remaining 22 chains. Ch 3, turn.

Row 2: Work 1 tr into each stitch to end of row. Ch 3 in colour B, turn.

Row 3: Using B work 1 tr into each stitch to end of row. Ch 3 in colour C, turn.

Row 4: Using C work 1 tr into each stitch to end of row. Ch 3 in colour B, turn.

Row 5: Using B work 1 tr into each stitch to end of row. Ch 3 in colour A, turn.

Row 6: Using A work 1 tr into each stitch to end of row. Ch 3, turn.

Row 7: Using A work 1 tr into each stitch to end of row.
Fasten off.

Making up

Sew in loose ends and place the two pieces wrong sides together. Using B and putting the hook through both pieces, work a row of double crochet down one long edge, along one short edge and up the other long edge. Fasten off.

Button loop

Using B, ch 26 sts, fasten off. Sew the loop in place to the inside centre of the back of the cosy. Sew on the button in a corresponding position to the front of the cosy.

Lining

Fold the piece of felt in half widthways and stitch down the two long edges. Place the lining inside the cozy and stitch the top edges together using slipstitch.

This fabulously soft, cozy scarf is quick and easy to knit in a chunky 2x2 rib. The two pockets make handy places to carry your phone or iPod and have button fastenings to keep them secure.

It's a wrap

Materials

Debbie Bliss Como (90% wool, 10% cashmere)
(46yd/42m per 50g ball)
6 x 50g balls of Blue
2 buttons
A pair of 10mm (UK000:US15) needles

Finished size

67 x 6in (170 x 15cm), not including fringe

Note

Yarn amounts given are based on average requirements and are approximate.

Tension

10 sts and 15 rows to 4in (10cm) over stocking stitch using 10mm needles.

Pocket back

Work 1 pocket back first.

Cast on 10 sts.

Row 1 (RS): P2, * k2, p2, rep from * to end.

Row 2: * K2, p2, rep from * to last 2 sts, K2.

These 2 rows set rib.

Continue until work measures 6in (15cm), ending with RS facing for next row.

Leave rem sts on a spare needle.

Scarf

Cast on 22 sts

Row 1 (RS): *K2 p2, rep from * to end k2.

Row 2: *P2, k2, rep from * to end, k2

These 2 rows set rib.

Work in rib for 11½in (30cm) ending with a WS row.

Make buttonhole

Next row: (K2, p2) twice, k2, yrn, p2tog, k2, work in rib to end of row.

Next row: Work in rib as set, knitting into the back of buttonhole st.

Work 2 more rows in rib.

Attach pocket back

Next row: K2, p2, k2, cast off next 10 sts in rib, fasten off yarn and rejoin to sts on RH needle, rib across the sts on the spare needle for the pocket back, keeping rib pattern correct to end of row.

Continue in 2 x 2 rib until work measures 43¼in (110cm) from the pocket top ending with a WS row.

Make second pocket

Next row (RS): K2, p2, k2, place the next 10 sts on a st holder, cast on 10 sts and rib across the remaining 6 sts.

Next row: Rib across all 22 sts keeping rib pattern correct.

Work 1 more row in rib.

Make buttonhole

Next row (WS): (P2, k2) twice, p2, yfwd k2tog, p2, work in rib to end of row. Continue in rib pattern until work measures the same as other end of scarf from pocket top to base of scarf.

Cast off.

Second pocket back

Rib across the 10 sts from the spare needle and keeping rib pattern correct continue until piece measures 6in (15cm).

Cast off.

Finishing off

Neatly stitch the pocket backs in place. Fasten the buttons on the scarf to correspond with the buttonholes on pockets.

Make fringes

Make 6 tassels for each end of the scarf measuring approximately 7in (18cm). Wrap the yarn around a piece of card that measures 8in (20cm) four times; cut through the bottom of the loops. Holding the top end of the loop, hook this through the bottom row of the scarf, pull the fringe end through the loop and pull tight. Repeat for the other end of the scarf.

This neat little pouch will store up to seven memory sticks, preventing them from getting lost at the bottom of your bag. The brightly patterned elephant is cut from a template and stitched onto the front.

Memory mate

Materials

6 x 4in (15 x 10cm) piece of patterned fabric
12 x 7in (30.5 x 18cm) piece of medium-weight
fabric x 2
12 x 4in (30.5 x 10cm) piece of medium-weight fabric
Small piece of felt in contrasting shade for elephant's ear
24in (61cm) length of ribbon, cut in half

Finished size

Approx. 11 x 7in (28 x 18cm) opened out
Approx. 4 x 5½in (10 x 12.75cm) closed

Elephant

1 Trace the diagram for the elephant, cut out a paper template and pin this to the patterned fabric; cut out the elephant shape. Cut out a small triangle of felt for the ear.

2 Stitch the ear on the elephant as shown on the right.

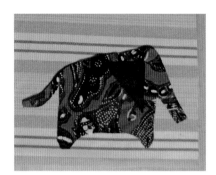

3 Pin the elephant onto the right side of one of the larger pieces of fabric, placing it ¾in (2cm) from the right-hand short edge and ¾in (2cm) from the bottom edge. Machine stitch on using satin stitch and a matching thread.

Pockets

4 Press, pin and stitch a ½in hem (1.5cm) along one long edge of the smaller piece of fabric. Place this on top of the larger piece of fabric without the elephant (both right sides facing up).

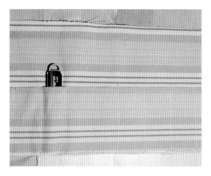

5 Place a pin ½in (1.5cm) in from each short edge, then 6 pins spaced at 1½in (4cm) intervals along the bottom edge. Repeat along the edge you have hemmed. The pins form the guide to stitch the pockets; stitch a straight line between each set of two pins to make 7 pockets.

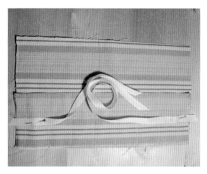

6 Place the piece of fabric you have just stitched with the pockets facing up. Pin the end of each ribbon to each side edge 1½in (4cm) from the bottom and roll the remaining ribbon up and place in the centre of the fabric.

7 Place the piece of fabric with the elephant face down on this and pin in place. Stitch all four edges leaving a 3in (8cm) gap on the bottom edge. Turn right side out through the gap, pushing out all the corners with a pencil. Hand sew the opening (see page 140) and press all the seams.

Flap

8 Make a flap by folding the top edge down by 2in (5cm) and press the fold line.

Finishing off

Fold the pouch in half so that the elephant sits squarely on the front and the ribbons meet. Press the fold line and tie the ribbons in a bow.

This subtly striped cozy makes a neat little case for a digital camera. It is knitted in warm shades of yarn and then felted in the washing machine to produce a strong piece of fabric that can be cut and sewn.

Stripes

Materials

Rowan Felted Tweed DK (191yd/175m per 50g ball)

1 x 50g ball each of Phantom (A), Rage (B), Bilberry (C), Pine (D) and Melody (E)

Crystal Palace Mikado Ribbon (112yd /102m per 50g ball)

Oddment of Jungle (F)

Oddment of Flame (G)

A pair of 4mm (UK8:US6) needles

4mm (UK8:USG/6) crochet hook

4in (10cm) Velcro

Finished size

5 x 3 x 1½in (12 x 8 x 4cm)

Note

Yarn amounts given are based on average requirements and are approximate.

Tension

22 sts and 30 rows to 4in (10cm) over stocking stitch using 4mm needles (before washing).

Main part

Cast on 60 sts and starting with a k row; continue in st st changing colours as follows:

Rows 1–8: A
Rows 9–19: C
Rows 20–21: F
Rows 22–23: C
Rows 24–27: A
Rows 28–32: B
Rows 33–34: F
Rows 35–44: E
Rows 45–46: G
Rows 47–49: D
Rows 50–56: E
Rows 57–59: F
Rows 60–61: B
Rows 62–72: C
Rows 73–74: G
Rows 75–76: B
Rows 77–80: A
Cast off.

Strap

Using the crochet hook, chain 50 sts. Fasten off.

Making up

Sew in all the loose ends. Machine wash the main piece of knitting and the strap at 60°C (it needs to felt enough to be able to cut and sew). When the felted piece is dry, cut one piece measuring 5 × 9in (12 × 23cm) (keeping one cast-on/cast-off edge widthways) and two pieces measuring 3½ × 2in (9 × 5cm) for the side panels. The stripes don't need to match up with the main part, but keep a cast-on/cast-off edge widthways. Place the larger piece face down with the cast-on cast-off edge at the bottom. Fold up the bottom third (diagram 1), place one side panel on top of this, right sides together (cast-on/cast-off edge at top), and stitch down the long edge (diagram 2), gently easing the main part to fit around the side panel. Continue stitching along the base and up the other side (following the line of stitches shown in the diagram). Repeat with the second side panel. Using the 4mm crochet hook and shade A work a row of double crochet around the flap; fasten off. Attach the strap to the back corner just inside the flap. If wanted, make a simple box lining as shown on page 140.

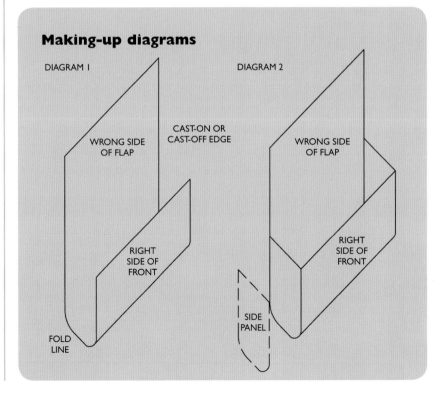

Making-up diagrams

DIAGRAM 1

WRONG SIDE OF FLAP

CAST-ON OR CAST-OFF EDGE

RIGHT SIDE OF FRONT

FOLD LINE

DIAGRAM 2

WRONG SIDE OF FLAP

RIGHT SIDE OF FRONT

SIDE PANEL

This design is utterly simple but ever so stylish. Quick and simple to make, it is an ideal introduction to knitting for novices and can be used to protect your mobile phone or your iPod.

Button up

Materials

Debbie Bliss Rialto DK (115yd/105m per 50g ball)

1 x 50g ball of Fuchsia

9 assorted buttons

A pair of 4mm (UK8:US6) needles

4mm (UK8:USG/6) crochet hook

10 x 3½in (26 x 9cm) piece of quilted lining fabric

Finished size

Approx. 5 x 3½in (13 x 9cm)

Note

Yarn amounts given are based on average requirements and are approximate.

TECHNO COZIES

Tension

22 sts and 42 rows over garter stitch using 4mm needles.

Front and back
(make 2 alike)

Cast on 30 sts, cont in g-st until piece measures 3½in (9cm); cast off.

Making up

Spacing the buttons evenly up the centre of the front piece, sew them into position. Place the two pieces of knitting together and neatly sew around the two long edges and one short edge in back stitch.

Loop

Using the 4mm crochet hook make a chain of 20 sts; fasten off. Sew the loop to the inside centre of the back piece so that it corresponds with the top button.

Lining

Turn each short edge of the lining fabric in to make a ½in (1.5cm) hem and stitch in place. Fold the fabric in half with right sides together; stitch down each long edge. Place the lining inside the knitted cozy, pushing the corners gently with a pencil or knitting needle. Using sewing thread, neatly slipstitch the lining in place around the inside of the opening.

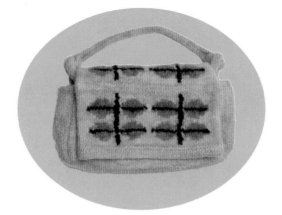

This cool, retro cozy is ideal for carrying a video camera. It is knitted using the intarsia method and then felted in the washing machine to make it sturdy. The case is lined with a quilted fabric for extra protection.

Retro

Materials
Fleece Artist Blue Face Aran 100% wool (202yd/185m per 125g skein)
1 x 125g ball each of Smoke (A) and Moss (B)
Oddment of Ebony (C)
19 x 13in (48 x 33cm) piece of quilted lining fabric
8in (20cm) Velcro

Size
12 x 6 x 4½in (31 x 15 x 11cm) before washing
9 x 5 x 3in (23 x 12 x 8cm) after washing

Note
Yarn amounts given are based on average requirements and are approximate.

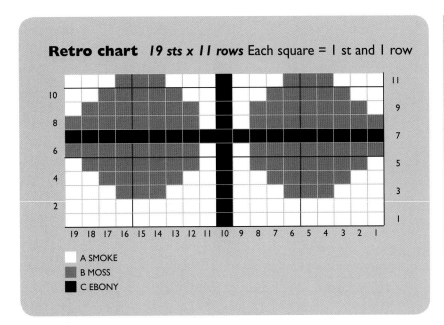

Retro chart *19 sts x 11 rows* Each square = 1 st and 1 row

- ☐ A SMOKE
- ▨ B MOSS
- ■ C EBONY

Tension

16 sts and 22 rows to 4in (10cm) over st st using 5mm needles (before washing).

Main part

Front panel

Using shade A cast on 50 sts.
Beg with a K row work 30 rows in st st, ending with a WS row.

Side panels and base

Next row (RS): Cast on 24 sts, knit to end of row (74 sts).
Next row: Cast on 24 sts, purl to end of row (98 sts).
Continue in st st for a further 24 rows, ending with a WS row.
Next row (RS): Cast off 24 sts, knit to end (74 sts).
Next row: Cast off 24 sts, purl to end (50 sts).

Back panel

Beg with a K row work 30 rows in st st, ending with a WS row.

Lid

* Knit 4 rows to form a g-st ridge.
Beg with a K row work 2 rows in st st.
Reading the chart from right to left on the knit rows and from left to right on the purl rows, work the pattern as follows:
Next row (RS): K5, work 1st row of chart, K2, repeat 1st row of chart, k5.
Next row: P5, work 2nd row of chart, p2, repeat 2nd row of chart, p5.

Continue as set until you have worked the 11-row pattern repeat twice.
Work 2 rows in st st. **

Front panel

Repeat from * to **, change to 4mm needles and work 6 rows in g-st.
Cast off.

Strap loops
(make 2 alike)

Using shade A cast on 6 sts and beg with a K row work in st st for 44 rows.
Cast off.

Strap

Using shade A cast on 6 sts and beg with a K row work in st st for 120 rows.
Cast off.

Finishing off

Sew in any loose ends. With right sides together, sew the side edges of the front panel to the cast-on sections of the side panels and base, then sew the cast-off edges of the side panels and base to the side edges of the back panel. This will form a box with a fold-over lid and front flap.

Sew each end of the strap loops inside the top corners of the side panels. Pull 3in (8cm) of one end of the long strap through one of the strap loops, double the strap over on itself and stitch

Lining diagram

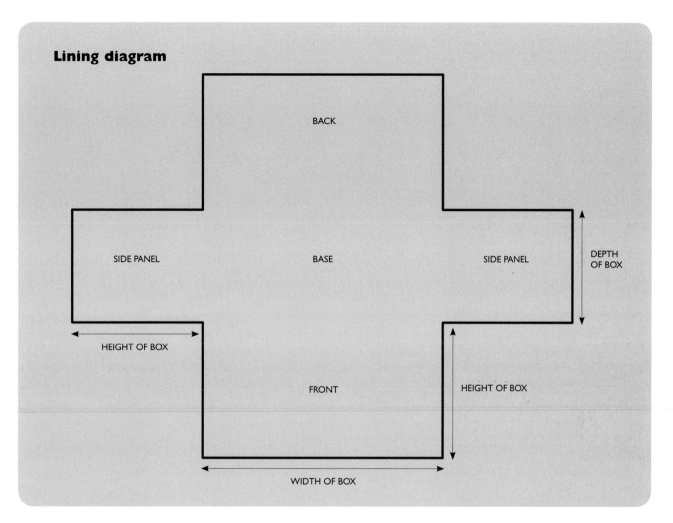

BACK

SIDE PANEL

BASE

SIDE PANEL

DEPTH OF BOX

HEIGHT OF BOX

FRONT

HEIGHT OF BOX

WIDTH OF BOX

in place; repeat with the other end. Machine wash at 60°C and gently pull into shape while still damp. If you can find a piece of wood or heavy book to mould the box around and leave it to dry, this will give crisper edges.

Lining

Measure the felted box and using these measurements cut a piece of lining fabric to the shape shown in the diagram. Fold and pin the side panels to meet the front and back panels (right sides together) as for the knitted piece. Stitch. Turn a ½in (1cm) hem out and stitch onto the wrong side of the lining. Place the lining inside the felted box and slipstitch into place.

Attach the Velcro to the inside of the bottom edge of the flap and the corresponding piece along the bottom edge of the front panel.

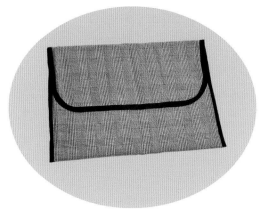

This ultra smart laptop case looks great in the office. It's made from classic tweed fabrics and has a padded lining, easy Velcro fastening and a simple bias-binding edging to complete it.

High-flyer

Materials

19 x 33in (48 x 84cm) piece of tweed fabric x 2
(matching or contrasting)
19 x 26in (48 x 66cm) piece of wadding
1yd (1m) bias binding 1in (2.5cm) width
10in (25cm) Velcro

Finished size

17 x 13in (43 x 33cm)

Main part

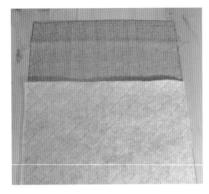

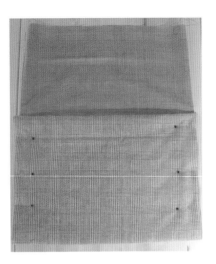

Flap

1 Place the two pieces of tweed fabric right sides together. Lay the wadding on top of this with one short edge lined up with the bottom short edge of the tweed fabrics.

2 Pin and baste all three fabrics together down both long edges and the bottom short edge leaving a 1in (2.5cm) seam allowance. Stitch and press the seams flat. Turn right side out, making sure that the wadding is sandwiched between the two tweed fabrics.

3 Press all the seams, then lay flat on the table with the outer tweed fabric right side down. Fold up the bottom 12½in (32cm) so that the bottom edge comes to where the wadding ends. Pin and baste the two side edges.

4 Stitch through all three fabrics with the right side of material facing.

5 Using a small plate as a guide, mark out a curve at each corner of the flap. Cut off the corners where marked.

6 Fold the bias binding in half lengthwise and press. Leaving an extra 1in (2.5cm) at each end of the bias binding, slot it over the side seams and around the edge of the flap, easing it around the curves. Pin in place, turning the extra 1in (2.5cm) at each end under to give a neat finish. Baste and stitch.

Finishing off

Press all the seams. Fasten the Velcro just inside the edge of the flap and in a corresponding position on the front of the cozy.

A great idea for the home office, this fabulous knitted hanging will cleverly disguise your computer screen when it's not in use. The chunky cables are knitted in creamy cotton to enhance the textured design.

Hide and seek

Materials

Debbie Bliss Cotton DK (92yd/84m per 50g ball) used double
7 x 50g balls of Ecru
A pair of 6mm (UK4:US10) needles
16 x 16in (41 x 41cm) piece of lining fabric

Finished size

16 x 23in (40.5 x 58cm) to fit an 18/19in (46/48cm) screen

Note

Yarn amounts given are based on average requirements and are approximate.

Tension

14 sts and 18 rows to 4in (10cm)
(using 2 strands of yarn together) over
stocking stitch using 6mm needles.

Special abbreviations

C4b – cable 4 at the back by placing
the next 2 sts onto the cable needle
and leaving at the back of work, k2,
then k2 from the cable needle

C4f – cable 4 at the front by placing 2
sts on the CN and leaving at the front
of work, k2, then k2 from the CN

Tw3b – twist 3 at the back by placing
the next st on the CN at the back of
work, k2, then p1 from CN

Tw3f – twist 3 at the front by placing
the next 2 sts on the CN at the front
of work, p1, then k2 from CN

Tw4b – twist 4 at the back by placing

the next 2 sts on the CN at the back
of work, k2, then p2 from CN

Tw4f – twist 4 at the front by placing
the next 2 sts on the CN at the front
of work, p2, then k2 from CN

Tw5b – twist 5 at the back by placing
the next 3 sts on the CN at the back
of work, k2, then p1, k2 from CN

Panel A

(24 sts)

Row 1 (RS): P2, C4b, (p4, C4b) twice, p2.

Row 2: K2, p4, (k4, p4) twice, k2.

Row 3: P1, Tw3b, (Tw4f, Tw4b) twice, Tw3f, p1.

Row 4: K1, p2, k3, p4, k4, p4, k3, p2, k1.

Row 5: Tw3b, p3, C4f, p4, C4f, p3, Tw3f.

Row 6: P2, k4, (p4, k4) twice, p2.

Row 7: K2, p3, Tw3b, Tw4f, Tw4b, Tw3f, p3, k2.

Row 8: (P2, k3) twice, p4, (k3, p2) twice.

Row 9: (K2, p3) twice, C4b, (p3, k2) twice.

Row 10: Repeat row 8.

Row 11: K2, p3, Tw3f, Tw4b, Tw4f, Tw3b, p3, k2.

Row 12: Repeat row 6.

Row 13: Tw3f, p3, C4f, p4, C4f, p3, Tw3b.

Row 14: Repeat row 4.

Row 15: P1, Tw3f, (Tw4b, Tw4f) twice, Tw3b, p1.

Row 16: Repeat row 2.

These 16 rows form the pattern.

TECHNO COZIES

Panel B

(17 sts)

Row 1 (RS): K2, p4, k2, p1, k2, p4, k2.

Row 2: K6, p2, k1, p2, k6.

Row 3: P6, Tw5b, p6.

Row 4: Repeat row 2.

Row 5: P5, Tw3b, k1, Tw3f, p5.

Row 6: K5, p2, k1, p1, k1, p2, k5.

Row 7: P4, Tw3b, k1, p1, k1, Tw3f, p4.

Row 8: K4, p2, k1, (p1, k1) twice, p2, k4.

Row 9: P3, Tw3b, k1, (p1, k1) twice, Tw3f, p3.

Row 10: K3, p2, k1, (p1, k1) 3 times, p2, k3.

Row 11: P2, Tw3b, k1, (p1, k1) 3 times, Tw3f, p2.

Row 12: K2, p2, k1, (p1, k1) 4 times, p2, k2.

Row 13: P1, Tw3b, k1 (p1, k1) 4 times, Tw3f, p1.

Row 14: K1, p2, k1, (p1, k1) 5 times, p2, k1.

Row 15: Tw3b, k1, (p1, k1) 5 times, Tw3f.

Row 16: P2, k1, (p1, k1) 6 times, p2.
These 16 rows form the pattern.

Front and back

Using 2 strands of yarn together cast on 60 sts and work in moss st as follows:

Row 1: * K1, p1, rep from * to end.

Row 2: * P1, k1, rep from * to end.
Repeat rows 1 and 2 once more, then repeat row 1.

Next row (WS): Moss 16, m1, moss 3, m1, moss 15, m1, (moss 3, m1) 4 times, moss 14 (67 sts).

Work Cable pattern as follows:

Row 1 (RS): Moss 4, p6, work row 1 of cable panel A, p6, work row 1 of cable panel B, p6, moss 4.

Row 2: Moss 4, k6, work cable panel B, k6, work cable panel A, k6, moss 4.

Row 3: Moss 4, p6, work cable panel A, p6, work cable panel B, p6, moss 4.

Row 4: Moss 4, k6, work cable panel B, k6, work cable panel A, k6, moss 4.
Continue to work the cable panels and keeping the stitch pattern correct and the beginning, centre and end of row as set until work measures 5in (12.5cm) ending with row 16 of the cable panels.

Next row (RS): Keeping moss st pattern correct work as follows: Moss 14, (patt2tog, moss 2) 4 times, patt2tog, moss 14, patt2tog, moss 2, patt2tog, moss 15 (60 sts).
Work 4 more rows in moss st.

To make fold line

Next row (WS): Knit.

Next row (RS): Knit.

Next row: Purl.
Continue in st st until work measures 5in (12cm) from the fold line, ending with a RS row.

Next row (WS): Knit.

Next row (RS): Knit.

Next row: Purl.
Continue in st st until work measures 2in (5cm) from the second fold line. Cast off.

Making up

Fold a 2in (5cm) hem at the second fold line and stitch in place. Stitch a ½in (1.5cm) hem on all 4 edges of the lining fabric, place the lining fabric and knitted piece wrong sides together, with the lining fabric at the back of the cable work, and stitch in place. The hanging will hook over the top of the computer. If necessary place a flat piece of wood or dowelling in the folded hem to balance the weight.

This knitted geometric design with crisp lines is perfect to protect your laptop. The hardwearing cotton denim shrinks after washing to form a firm fabric. For extra protection, line it with a basic quilted fabric.

Mitre

Materials

Rowan Denim (109yd/100m per 50g ball)

5 × 50g balls of Dark Blue (A)

3 × 50g balls of Ecru (B)

A pair of 4mm (UK8:US6) needles

A pair of 3.75mm (UK9:US5) needles

12in (30cm) Velcro

16 × 24in (41 × 61cm) piece of quilted lining fabric

12 × 1½in (31 × 4cm) piece of quilted lining fabric × 2

Finished size

Approx. 16 × 12 × 1½in (41 × 31 × 4cm) after washing

Note

Yarn amounts given are based on average requirements and are approximate.

Tension

20 sts and 28 rows to 4in (10cm) over garter st (before washing).

Note

This design is worked in garter stitch stripes, changing the colour every two rows. The yarn can be carried up at the side of the work and does not need to be cut at the end of every alternate row.

Front and back section A
(make 2 alike)

Using yarn A and 4mm needles cast on 100 sts.

Rows 1 & 2: Knit.

Row 3 (RS): Using yarn B k58, (k2tog) twice, k38 (98 sts).

Row 4 and every alt row: Knit using appropriate yarn.

Row 5: Using yarn A k57, (k2tog) twice, k37 (96 sts).

Row 7: Using yarn B k56, (k2tog) twice, k36 (94 sts).

Row 9: Using yarn A k55, (k2tog) twice, k35 (92 sts).

Continue decreasing in this way, working 1 stitch less before and after the two decreases and changing the shade every 2 rows, until you have 24 sts remaining.

Next row: K20, (k2tog) twice (22 sts).
Next row: K22.
Cast off rem 22 sts.

Front and back section B
(make 2 alike)
Using yarn A and 4mm needles cast on 100 sts.
Rows 1 & 2: Knit.
Row 3 (RS): Using yarn B K38, (k2tog) twice, k58 (98 sts).
Row 4 and every alt row: Knit using appropriate yarn.
Row 5: Using yarn A K37, (k2tog) twice, k57 (96 sts).
Row 7: Using yarn B K36, (k2tog) twice, k56 (94 sts).
Row 9: Using yarn A K35, (k2tog) twice, k55 (92 sts).
Continue decreasing in this way, working 1 stitch less before and after the two decreases and changing the shade every 2 rows, until you have 24 sts remaining.
Next row: (K2tog) twice, k20 (22 sts).
Next row: K22.
Cast off rem 22 sts.

Side panels, base panel and strap
Using A and 4mm needles cast on 12 sts.
Row 1: Sl 1, k11.
This row sets pattern.

Continue until work measures 71in (180cm).
Cast off.

Band for Velcro
Using A and 4mm needles cast on 8 sts.
Row 1: Sl 1, k7.
This row sets pattern.
Continue until work measures 30in (76cm).
Cast off.

Making up
Lay front section A and front section B flat and using mattress stitch, sew up centre seam (see diagram). Do the same for sections A and B of the back. Using shade A and 3.75mm needles pick up and knit 78 sts along the cast-on edge (top) of front, knit 1 row. Cast off. Repeat for back.

Wash all the pieces separately and gently stretch into shape while damp.

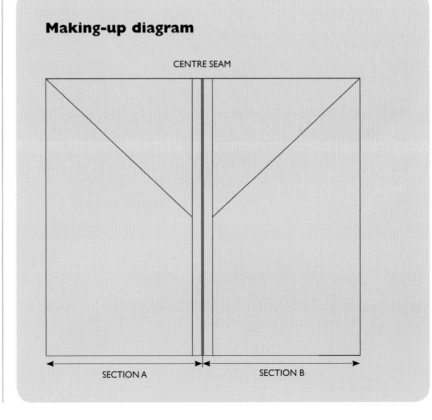

Making-up diagram

CENTRE SEAM

SECTION A

SECTION B

Sew the two short ends of the long strap/side/base panel together to make a continuous loop. With right sides together and using backstitch attach the loop down one short edge, along the bottom edge and up the other short edge of the front panel, easing it around the corners as you sew. Repeat with the back panel. This should leave you with a carrying strap of approximately 25in (64cm).

Sew the knitted band up the centre seam of the back panel. Attach one side of the Velcro to the centre seam of the front panel and the corresponding Velcro to the inside of the knitted band to fasten it to the front panel.

Lining

Stitch a hem at both short ends of the larger piece of lining fabric for the front and back panel and hem one short end of each of the smaller pieces of lining fabric for the side panels. Fold the front and back panel in half so that the hemmed edges are at the top. With right sides together and all hemmed edges at the top, pin the side panels in place along each open edge, easing them around the corners. Stitch. Place the lining inside the knitted cozy and slipstitch in place along the top edge.

This pretty, eye-catching cozy is a fun and stylish way to carry an iPad. It is knitted in a beautiful, soft multicoloured yarn and embellished with a simple leaf design, then felted in the washing machine.

Purple haze

Materials

Rowan Colourscape Chunky 100% lambswool (175yd/160m per 100g skein)

2 x 100g skeins of shade 432 Heath (A)

Rowan Kidsilk Aura 75% kid mohair/25% silk (82yd/75m per 25g ball)

1 x 25g ball of Forest (B)

A pair each of 4mm (UK8:US6) and 7mm (UK2:US10.5) needles

18 x 13in (46 x 33cm) piece of lining fabric

2 press studs

Size

17 x 11½in (43 x 29cm) before washing

Approx. 13 x 9in (33 x 23cm) after washing

Note

Yarn amounts given are based on average requirements and are approximate.

TECHNO COZIES

Tension (before washing)

14 sts and 18 rows to 4in (10cm) over stocking stitch using yarn A and 7mm needles.

20 sts and 19 rows to 4in (10cm) over stocking stitch using yarn B and 4mm needles.

Front and back

Using yarn A and 7mm needles, cast on 60 sts.
Work 2 rows in g-st.
Beg with a K row, continue in st st until work measures 11.5in (29cm), ending with a RS row.
Next row (WS): K (to form ridge).
Beg with a K row, continue in st st until work measures the same as front to g-st edging, ending with a WS row.
Work 2 rows in g-st.
Cast off.

Handles
(make 2 alike)

Using yarn A and 7mm needles, cast on 80 sts.
Work 6 rows in g-st.
Cast off.

Leaves
(make 6 alike)

Using yarn B and 4mm needles cast on 3 sts.
Row 1 (RS): K1, yfwd, k1, yfwd, k1 (5 sts).
Row 2 and every foll alt row: P.
Row 3: K2, yfwd, k1, yfwd, k2 (7 sts).
Row 5: K3, yfwd, k1, yfwd, K3 (9 sts).
Row 7: K4, yfwd, k1, yfwd, K4 (11 sts).
Row 8: Purl.
Work 2 rows in st st.
Next row: K1, k2 tog tbl, k to last 3 sts, k2 tog, k1.
This row sets decreases.
Repeat decrease row on every 4th row until 5 stitches remain.
Next row: K1, k3 tog, k1 (3 sts).
Purl 1 row.
Next row: Sl 1, k2 tog, psso.
Fasten off.

Making up

Sew the leaves in position in the bottom right-hand corner of the front half of bag just above the fold line (see image). Using yarn B embroider a chain-stitch stem between the leaves.

Fold the cozy in half at the fold line and join the side seams with mattress stitch. Fasten each end of the handles 2in (5cm) in from the side edges of the front and back. Machine wash at 40°C. Gently stretch into shape while damp.

Make a basic lining and stitch in place (see page 140). Attach the 2 press studs 3in (8cm) in from the side edges where the lining meets the garter-stitch edging.

Techniques

How to make your gadgets great!

Materials

The materials stated for each design may be substituted with different brands and types. However, it is advisable to use natural fibres wherever possible since this reduces the amount of static build-up on your gadget.

Felting

Ensure that the yarn or recycled garment you are using is suitable for felting and always machine wash a test swatch before commencing at the recommended temperature. Suitable yarns to use are pure wool (instructions on the label should be for hand washing and NOT machine washing), mohair and alpaca or a blend of any of these three.

Knitting and crochet

It is best to use pure wool or pure cotton. If substituting with a different brand, check the yardage and tension given against the details on the ball band of the yarn you want to use.

If necessary, use larger or smaller needles to obtain correct tension. In the patterns, colour names are given in capitals if they are actual shade names.

Sewing

Medium-weight dressmaking or household fabrics in wool, cotton or linen are suitable for the projects in this book. Standard sewing thread in a shade that matches the fabric can be used for all the projects unless otherwise stated.

Basic equipment

- Knitting needles
- Crochet hooks
- Wool needle
- Sewing needle
- Tapestry needle
- Leather sewing needle
- Tape measure
- Straight edge/metal rule
- Scissors

Felting technique

Machine felting

Ensure that the yarn used in the piece to be felted will shrink and is not machine washable. Suitable fibres are pure wool, mohair and alpaca. Some modern pure wools have been treated to make them machine washable and are not suitable; they tend to feel smoother since the fibres have been flattened.

When you are knitting a piece to felt always try a test square. Make a note of the number of stitches and rows to the square and the measurements, machine wash the test piece at 40° in the washing machine and gently stretch into shape to dry it. If you want further shrinkage then wash it again at 60°.

Helpful tips for machine felting

Put the pieces to be felted in the washing machine with something that will cause more friction such as jeans or a pair of trainers. Use a detergent since this will speed up the felting process and help to mat the fibres.

When you take the fabric out of the washing machine gently stretch it into shape while it is still damp.

If it is a bag that has already been sewn up try to find a similar-shaped object that you can mould it around to dry; this will create neater edges.

Sewing techniques

All the patterns in this book are stitched with a sewing machine unless stated otherwise, with a small amount of hand sewing to finish.

Basting or tacking

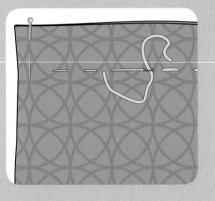

This is used to hold two pieces of fabric together temporarily using large running stitches. Place the right sides together and fasten the sewing thread. Working from right to left, bring the needle up through the fabric, then back down through the fabric making a straight stitch. Continue to the end of the piece of fabric keeping the stitches the same size and distance apart.

Hemming

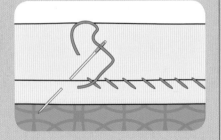

This makes a neat edge to your fabric by turning the raw edge under and stitching with a sewing machine or by hand. If stitching by hand, fold the fabric twice to make the hem and work from right to left with the wrong side facing.

Straight seam

A plain straight seam is used to fasten two pieces of fabric. The stitches remain an even distance from the edge of the fabric all the way down the seam.

Rounded corners

When you reach the corner of the fabric, stop with the needle in the fabric, lift the machine foot and turn the fabric to bring the next straight edge in line, drop the foot and continue stitching to the next corner.

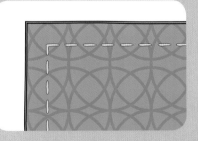

Appliqué

This is a way of embellishing your projects with fabric shapes to make a unique design. The embellishment can be hand or machine stitched using simple straight stitch or more elaborate embroidery stitches.

Satin stitch or zigzag

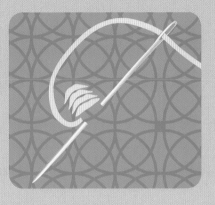

A long, decorative, straight stitch used to fasten a raw edge of fabric.

Box pleats

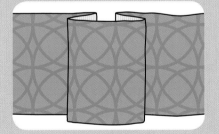

Pleats are folds in the fabric that create a concertina effect. The fabric is folded and pressed at regular intervals to create a series of straight folds.

Cross-stitch

This is an embroidery stitch used for embellishment and is usually worked on aida, a block-weave fabric with a hole at the corner of each block. The stitch is made by bringing the needle from the back of the fabric to the front through the bottom-left hole, then from the front of the fabric to the back through the top-right hole, then from the back of the fabric to the front through the bottom-right hole and from the front of the fabric to the back through the top-left hole.

Basic lining

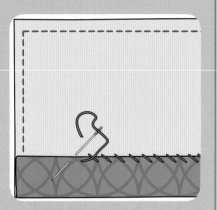

Measure your finished cozy and cut the lining fabric to measure the same length + ¾in (2cm) x double the width + ½in (1cm). Fold the lining in half widthways with right sides together; stitch a seam along the base and up the side edge. Press the seam flat. Turn down a hem along the top edge and stitch in place. Place the lining inside the cozy and neatly stitch in place along the top edge.

Back stitch

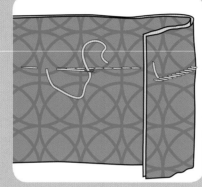

Place the two pieces to be stitched wrong sides together. Working from right to left, fasten the thread and bring the needle from the underneath through to the top side, place the needle back through the fabric a small distance to the right, then bring back up a small distance to the left of the first stitch. Place the needle back in the hole at the front of the first stitch and bring back through the fabric a stitch length to the left. Continue to the end of the row.

Overstitch

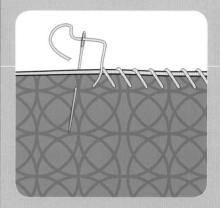

This is mainly used in the patterns to fasten a lining to the inside of a cozy or to sew up openings. With the two pieces of fabric in place, work a small neat stitch between the two, just catching each piece of fabric with the thread and running the thread behind the fabric between stitches.

Running stitch

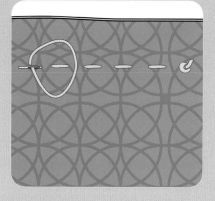

This is the same as tacking or basting but a smaller stitch is created. Fasten the thread and working from the right to the left of the work weave the needle in and out of the fabric a few times in a straight line before pulling the thread through; this will form a row of small straight stitches. Keep the size of the stitches and the gaps the same.

French knot

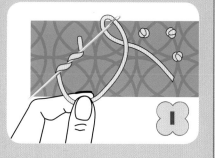

1 This method of embroidery creates a raised bobble. Secure the thread on the wrong side of your work and pass the needle through to the right side. Wrap the thread around the needle a few times then re-insert the needle into the same hole.

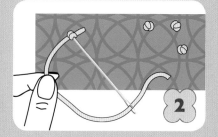

2 Gently pull it to tighten the thread and fasten off on the wrong side of your work.

Slip stitch

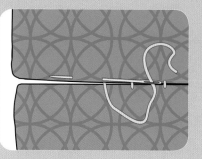

This is used to join two folded edges or to fasten a lining inside a knitted project. Fasten the thread and working from right to left bring the needle up through one folded edge and then back through the other piece of fabric to make a tiny stitch. Continue along the row, running the thread between the fold so that it doesn't show.

Crochet techniques

Slip knot

Hold the yarn in your left hand looped over the index finger and supported by the thumb and middle finger. Hold the hook in your right hand, between the thumb, index finger and middle finger.

Insert the crochet hook through the loop of yarn from right to left, twist the hook in a complete turn and then hook the ball-end yarn through the loop and tighten; this forms the slip knot.

Chain stitch (ch) This is the foundation row for crochet.

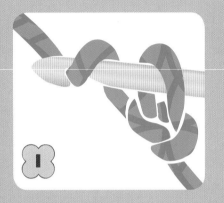

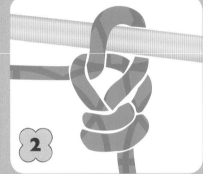

1 With the crochet hook in your right hand make a slip knot. Hold the slip knot in your left hand and insert the crochet hook into the slip knot from front to back. Hook the yarn through; this completes the first chain st.

2 Hook another loop through the chain st and draw it through. Repeat until you have the required amount of chain sts.

Double crochet (dc)

1 Place the crochet hook into the next stitch or space to be worked, wrap the yarn over the crochet hook and draw the loop through the stitch on the work.

2 You now have two stitches on the hook. Wrap the yarn over the hook and draw through both stitches leaving one stitch on the hook.

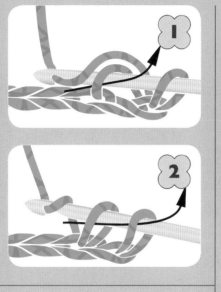

Half treble (h-tr)

1 Wrap the yarn over the hook and insert hook in the next stitch or space to be worked, wrap the yarn over hook again and draw through the work only (three loops on the hook).

2 Wrap the yarn over the hook again and draw through all three loops.

Treble (tr)

1 Wrap the yarn over the hook and insert hook in the next stitch or space to be worked, wrap the yarn over the hook again and draw through the work only (three loops on the hook).

2 Wrap the yarn over the hook and draw through the first two loops on the hook. Then wrap the yarn over the hook and draw through the remaining two loops on the hook.

Knitting techniques

Casting on

There are a number of methods for casting on; two of the most common are the thumb method and cable method.

Thumb method

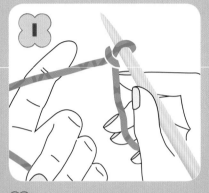

1 Holding the needle in the right hand make a slip knot leaving approximately 1yd (1m) of yarn at the end of the loop. Place the loop on the needle.

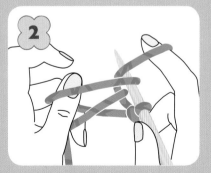

2 Wrap the tail end of yarn around the thumb and place the needle through the loop.

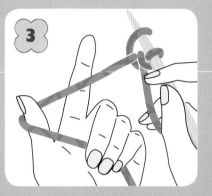

3 Draw the yarn attached to the ball through the loop and place the new loop on the needle. This is your first stitch. Repeat until you have the specified amount of stitches on the needle.

Cable method

1 Make a slip knot and place the loop on the needle in the left hand.

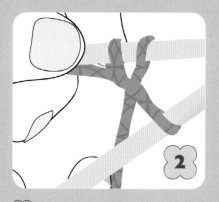

2 Knit into this stitch making another loop, which you place on the same needle.

3 Insert the right-hand needle between the 2 stitches on the left-hand needle, wrap the yarn around the right and needle and bring the loop through to the front of work and place it on the point of the left-hand needle.

4 Continue to insert the right-hand needle between the two stitches nearest the point of the left-hand needle and place the new loop at the point of the needle. Repeat until you have the specified amount of stitches on the needle.

Casting off

1 Knit the first two stitches from the left-hand needle, then pass the first stitch on the right-hand needle over the stitch nearest the point of the needle.

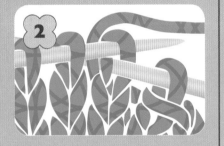

2 Knit the next stitch. Pass the first stitch on the right-hand needle over the stitch nearest the point of the needle. Repeat to end of row. When you have just one stitch left on the needle, pull it gently to make a larger loop. Cut the yarn, pass through the loop, pull tight.

Knit stitch

1 Hold the needle with the cast-on stitches in your left hand. Keeping the yarn at the back of work place the point of the needle in your right hand through the loop of the first stitch on the left-hand needle.

2 Wrap the yarn in between the two needlepoints and draw through the loop.

3 Place the resulting loop on the right-hand needle. This is your first stitch. Repeat to the end of the row.

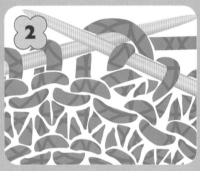

Purl stitch

1 Place the needle with all the stitches in your left hand. Holding the yarn at the front of work, place the point of the right-hand needle into the front edge of the first stitch (the side nearest to the point of the needle).

2 Wrap the yarn around the point of the right-hand needle and pull the loop through.

3 Place the new stitch on the right-hand needle. Repeat to the end of the row.

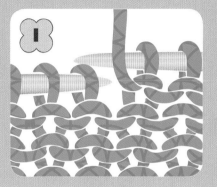

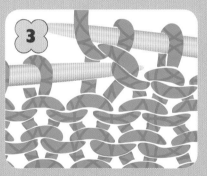

Ⓐ Garter stitch

The easiest stitch of all, every row is worked in the knit stitch. This forms a ridge that is ideal for scarves and blankets, since it does not curl at the edges.

Ⓑ Stocking stitch

This is the most popular stitch in knitting and consists of one row knit stitch (right side of work) and one row purl (wrong side of work). Reverse stocking stitch is worked in exactly the same way, but the purl row is the right side of work.

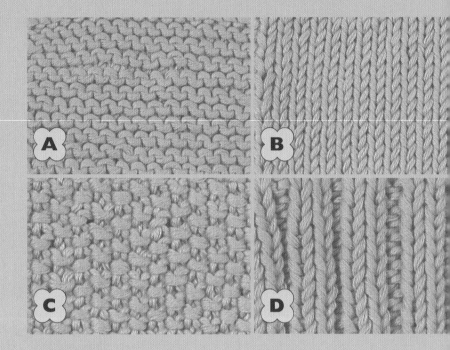

Ⓒ Moss stitch

This forms a textured piece that lies flat without curling at the edges. It is formed by working knit 1, purl 1 to the end of the first row and starting the next row with the same stitch that you ended on. For example, if you ended the previous row with a purl stitch you will start the next row with a purl stitch and work p1, k1 to the end.

Ⓓ Rib

Ribbing forms a firm, slightly gathered edge to knitting, normally used at the base of a sweater and for cuffs and necklines. It can be formed by different numbers of stitches, 1x1 rib (see 'D') is 1 knit stitch and 1 purl stitch to the end of the row, 2x2 rib is 2 knit stitches and 2 purl stitches to the end of the row etc. If you end the row with a purl stitch you will start the next row with a knit stitch and if you end the row with a knit stitch you will start the next row with a purl stitch; this forms a pattern of vertical ridges.

Cable

 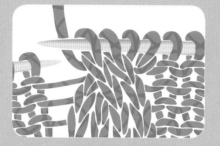 

Cabling is worked by placing a number of stitches onto a cable needle at the front or back of work; the next group

of stitches on the left-hand needle are knitted, then the stitches from the cable needle are knitted, forming a

textured plait. There are many cable patterns; these will be explained in each pattern with a set of abbreviations.

Fair Isle

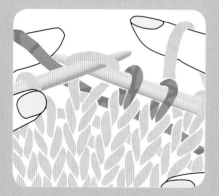

Fair-isle is used when knitting a regular pattern with two or more colours in blocks of up to five or six stitches. The spare yarn is stranded loosely at the back of work and woven in every third stitch by crossing it over the yarn currently in use. Fair Isle is usually worked from a chart in stocking stitch; the knit rows are read from right to left and the purl rows from left to right.

Intarsia

This is used when knitting large blocks of colour in one row. Each colour block has a separate ball of yarn wound onto a bobbin to avoid tangles; when you change colour, cross the previous shade over the strand of the new shade to avoid any holes.

Increasing

A Knit into the next stitch on the left-hand needle and before slipping it off the needle knit into the back of the stitch as well and place the two stitches on the right-hand needle.

B Alternatively, pick up the strand of yarn that is lying between the stitch just worked and the next stitch on the left-hand needle, knit into the back of this loop and place on the right-hand needle.

Knit into front and back of next stitch

Make one

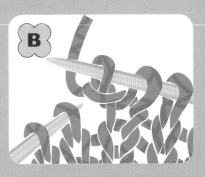

Decreasing

A Place the right-hand needle into the second stitch from the point of the left-hand needle and also through the first stitch so that you knit them both together at the same time. This decrease can also be worked on a purl row in exactly the same way but by purling the two stitches together.

B Alternatively, slip the next stitch from the left-hand needle to the right-hand needle without knitting it, knit the next stitch then pass the slip stitch over the stitch nearest the point of the right-hand needle as if you are casting off.

Knit two stitches together   Pass slip stitch over

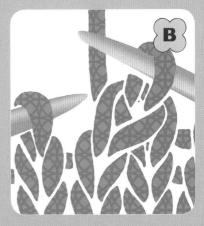

Beading

 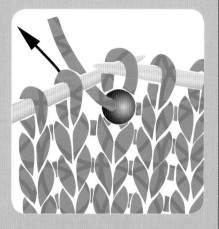

Beads can be incorporated into knitting by threading them onto the yarn before starting to knit. Thread a fine beading needle with sewing thread and fasten in a large loop. Place the end of the knitting yarn through the loop and thread the beads onto the needle, pushing them down onto the knitting yarn. To place the beads on the knitting, bring the yarn with the bead to the front of work, slip the next st, place the bead in front of the slipped stitch, pulling the yarn taut then work the next st as instructed.

Mattress stitch

This is a neat seam for sewing together two pieces of knitting. Place the knitted pieces to be adjacent on a flat surface with right sides facing up. Attach the yarn at the base, place the needle under the horizontal bar between the first and second stitch on the right-hand piece, then in the same position on the left-hand piece. Continue up the join, weaving in and out to form a ladder. Pull the yarn tight, and this will form an invisible seam.

Abbreviations

Knitting

alt	alternate	**p**	purl
beg	beginning	**patt**	pattern
CN	cable needle	**psso**	pass slip stitch over
cont	continue	**p2tog**	purl 2 sts together
dec	decrease by knitting 2 sts together	**RS**	right side
DPN	double-pointed needle	**sll**	slip one stitch without knitting it
g-st	garter stitch	**st(s)**	stitch(es)
inc	increase by knitting into the front and back of next st	**st st**	stocking stitch
		tbl	through back loops
k	knit	**tog**	together
k2tog	knit 2 sts together	**WS**	wrong side
k3tog	knit 3 sts together	**yfwd**	yarn forward
ml	make 1 by picking up the horizontal bar between the stitches on each needle and knitting into the back of it	**yon**	yarn over needle
		yrn	yarn round needle

Crochet

ch	chain
dc	double crochet
htr	half treble crochet
sl st	slip stitch
tr(s)	treble(s) crochet
yo	yarn over

Conversions

Needle sizes

UK	Metric	US
14	2mm	0
13	2.5mm	1
12	2.75mm	2
11	3mm	ñ
10	3.25mm	3
ñ	3.5mm	4
9	3.75mm	5
8	4mm	6
7	4.5mm	7
6	5mm	8
5	5.5mm	9
4	6mm	10
3	6.5mm	10.5
2	7mm	10.5
1	7.5mm	11
0	8mm	11
00	9mm	13
000	10mm	15

Crochet hook sizes

UK /Canada	Metric	US	UK/Canada	Metric	US
14	2	–	7	4.5	–
13	2.25	B/1	6	5	H/8
12	2.5	–	5	5.5	I/9
–	2.75	C/2	4	6	J/10
11	3	–	3	6.5	K/10.5
10	3.25	D/3	2	7	–
9	3.5	E/4	0	8	L/11
–	3.75	F/5	00	9	M/13
8	4	G/6	000	10	N/15

UK/US yarn weights

UK	US	UK	US
2-ply	Lace	Aran	Fisherman's worsted
3-ply	Fingering	Chunky	Bulky
4-ply	Sport	Super chunky	Extra bulky
Double knitting	Light worsted		

About the author

Sue Culligan owns Kangaroo, a mail-order supply company for knitting yarns and accessories. She designs a range of knitting kits for the KnitKits label, writes the yarn review for *Knitting Magazine* and is the author of *The Knitting Stitch and Motif Directory*. Sue lives in south-west France, where she runs a *Chambre d'hôte*, knitting retreats and knitting and crochet workshops.

Acknowledgements

I would like to say a huge, huge thank you to the following – my family and friends for putting up with me, feeding me and generally looking after me during the creation of *Techno Cozies*, especially my wonderful husband. To Kim for her help with some of the sewing, Frances, Jo and Wendy from my knitting group for making up some of the knitting and crochet projects and last but not least Sarah Hatton for all her patient pattern checking.

Sources

Buttons, knitting needles and accessories
www.kangaroo.uk.com

Fleece Artist
www.fleeceartist.com

Crystal Palace yarns
www.straw.com

Jamieson & Smith Shetland Wool
www.shetlandwoolbrokers.co.uk

Debbie Bliss and Noro Yarns
www.designeryarns.uk.com

Rowan Yarns
www.knitrowan.com

Index

To place an order, or to request a catalogue, contact:

GMC Publications Ltd

Castle Place, 166 High Street, Lewes, East Sussex, BN7 1XU

United Kingdom

Tel: +44 (0)1273 488005   **Fax:** +44 (0)1273 402866

Website: www.gmcbooks.com

Orders by credit card are accepted